PERFUMED STEAMROLLER

A Journey into the
World of Technology

Christine McNamara

Published in Australia in 2017 by Christine McNamara

Email: perfumedsteamroller2017@gmail.com
Web: www.perfumedsteamroller.com.au

ISBN 9780648100706 (paperback)

A catalogue record for this book is available from the National Library of Australia

Disclaimer

The author has made every effort to ensure the accuracy of the information within this book was correct at the time of publication. The author does not assume and hereby disclaims any liability to any party for any loss, damage or disruption caused by errors or omissions, whether such errors or omissions result from accident, negligence, or any other cause.

Contents

Preface

I initially decided to write this book while I was on my way home from Russia following my usual birthday rendezvous with my girlfriends – my group of travelling buddies who have always inspired me. On the flight over, I read a book called *The Aging Myth* by Joseph Chang, PhD on anti-aging (hey, I am a girl after all!) and I thought to myself that if a scientist could write a book that I could easily get my head around, then so could I. I was inspired by the format and approach Dr Chang had used in *The Aging Myth*. For many years it had been my dream to put down on paper my experiences working in the world of technology over the past three decades.

This book was born out of my long career experience and many years as a contractor in charge of different technology projects for various organisational teams. While my own experience centres on the technology industry, I wanted to avoid becoming too technical and using too much jargon in the pages of this book. Many of the career success advice and tips I share are applicable across multiple industries and many kinds of businesses. If you work with people, if you

are involved in implementing processes, if you juggle partners (including customers and vendors), if you seek to drive
change and improvement through various projects, or if you
use tools and technology to achieve results, then this book is
for you.

What you will discover in these pages are the experiences of a woman, who focused on delivering exceptional
service (beyond anyone's expectation) in a traditionally male-
dominated work environment by living in the shoes of the
customer. And, as many people would agree, this process of
striving to achieving perfection came at a personal cost.

My hope is that you will find the experiences and
information I describe in this book to be useful and thought-
provoking and that it will help you to come up with new and
interesting ways to make a difference in your world.

Christine McNamara
November 2017

Introduction

Launching into a Career in Technology

It all really started for me back in the 1970s when my father brought home our first computer – a Commodore 64 – and I learned to type 'the quick brown fox jumped over the lazy dog' over and over until I was a proficient touch typist. In 1981, my father brought an Apple II Europlus as Apple had expanded its distribution into Australia in 1978 and these computers were starting to become readily available.

With its dual floppies and running a Sandy word processor, this Apple II Europlus was to last me until I'd completed a Computing and Management Information Systems degree by correspondence in 1990. The reason that I decided to study this degree in the first place was because one of my brothers had told me that I would earn $10,000 more per year if I had a degree … and who ever said it wasn't all about the money!

After having worked in administration and accounting jobs for four years, I started working in the technology field in July 1986, using a Wang and Phillips mini-computer. These machines were a step down from a mainframe computer and they had the necessary 'grunt' to process large amounts of data – usually for invoicing purposes and, of course, processing financials. It wasn't until later on that I realised what an asset a strong financial background would be to my career path.

At the time, I had to convert from CPM on the Apple II to DOS on an IBM PC and from the big disk spindles to 8 inch and then to 5¼ inch floppies with the advent of 10MB hard drives in the market. It was while I was studying for my degree that I launched myself into the technology world and discovered that my talents lay in systems analysis and design which, once again, I was oblivious of the benefits until further down the track. But, at this point, I was off and running.

Over the next eight years, I worked for three different companies until I decided that there was more money to be made in being a contractor rather than in management – particularly if you were female and extremely technical.

Think I'm 'Just a Girl'? Think Again!

My first appreciation for being an anomaly in IT as a result of my gender occurred when I attended a technical seminar to check out Retix routers – a new type of network technology – in 1989. The seminar was being held at a secure building so each registered attendee had to present themselves to the front office when they arrived. When I walked up to the glass window to sign-in for the seminar, the lady said to me, 'You must be Christine McNamara'. You can imagine how surprised I was! When I walked into the seminar room her comment made sense since, of the 50 attendees, I was the *only female*. I strolled up to the front of the room and sat in the front row and away we went.

Up to this point, I had been the Technical guru and the first employee of a start-up technology business so I had no idea that being female was … well … odd. The situation only started to heat up when I moved into my first corporate IT role.

There were many firsts as a female for me during those early years: working as a Wide Area Network (WAN) and Local Area Network (LAN) engineer with qualifications in cabling, OTDR (fibre testing), Retix Routing, Novell SFT III, SCO Unix and with just about every networking and desktop product on the market, with new ones emerging weekly. I was responsible for installing them in small- to medium-sized businesses all over Sydney and country NSW as quickly as my boss and his partner could sell them. Of course, the subsequent challenge was to then support these IT systems so I took on the task of building my first support business and designing my first support procedure in 1990.

Setting up a services organisation was my very first challenge. It involved teaching people to move from manual ledgers to computers … and there were some hard nuts to crack! Over the following 20 years (1994–2014), I was involved in the implementation of 25 projects across 21 organisations – essentially doing the same thing in each business (moving them from A to B). During that time, everything changed except one thing – people are still the same.

So What Do I Know Now?

In reflecting back over these 25 projects, I am aware of many similarities between them even though the projects incorporated vastly different characteristics. The one common theme was that they all were delivered on time (or in a shorter timeframe), to budget (or less) and achieved the outcomes I was commissioned to deliver (or more) using the people, processes, partners, project methods and technology available to me.

Having delivered projects in 21 different organisations, I've experimented with most approaches in order to achieve optimal results. As a result, I have conclusively discovered that the key factor is to collect all the *data* to ensure that I have buy-in and *Executive sponsorship*. While I learnt that it wasn't always possible to reach a consensus during the project delivery (and that's where tough decisions need to be made), having supporting data with executive sponsorship made all the difference.

THE 4PT Framework – Putting All the Pieces into Place

During the course of my career – after having put all of the basics in place and introduced a common language – I eventually realised that there are many lenses to look through when building an IT operation/business. Consequently, I came up with the concept of a framework to explain my insights and knowledge to others – the 4PT Framework which focuses on People, Process, Partners, Projects and Technology and the integration of these parameters. In the pages of this book, you will find out about this process and how it could be beneficial to your own career or business.

When you do what you are passionate about for long enough you discover there is a science to it!

The 4PT Framework: PEOPLE

CHAPTER 1

Inspiring Job Satisfaction:
Chart progress towards a shared goal

The people you have working in your team, operation, or business are the most important aspect to Service Integration and Management. Once you have experienced working with a great team, there is nothing sweeter and more enjoyable, regardless of the size of the goal.

As an IT Manager, this process starts with the basics: Position Descriptions, Special Projects, what to do with Over-achievers, and Skills Profiling.

My biggest learning from working with a great team is that people working together can achieve extraordinary outcomes that might have seemed impossible to accomplish without exactly the right mix of skills, ideas, and personalities.

I specifically focus on aspects of people management that are driven by delivering an agreed-upon outcome within a fixed period of time. Where I have not had a deadline provided for me, I have simply created my own. I believe that without progress towards a goal, people will not be satisfied in their jobs – and even if they don't initially agree or understand the concept consciously, most seem to get it in the end.

Dealing with IT people who are mostly introverts is not for the fainthearted. But over the course of my career, I've identified many operational aspects of Service Integration and Management I believe have wide application, so I'll share those with you here. But before we dive in, for all the non-IT people out there, I first must apologise for the way we IT people talk. Like any industry, we've developed a short-hand language (or jargon) to converse amongst ourselves. In the case of the IT industry, this language is very short; we're talking about using three or four letters to describe a complex topic by means of acronyms. Just call us concise and efficient!

Position Descriptions

Having a detailed and accurate description for each position – a Position Description (PD) – signals commitment to each person from the management level. If as an IT Manager or Team Leader you cannot detail an employee's or contractor's role and what exactly you expect from them, then how can that person meet or exceed your expectations? Clarifying roles and expectations – and even the process of discussing this with each person on your team – quickly improves performance levels.

I consider this personal attention to be key to moving from manager to leader. It is a skill that is necessary to enable a team to attain set goals. I have found the top performers who want to exceed expectations must have clear goals and know what they are contributing to. Tapping into this desire to achieve and this horsepower it makes available to you very early on will make life so much easier for the whole team.

Throughout my career I have made a point of getting to know HR departments very well, and I always spend my initial period at any organisation obtaining a structure chart, ensuring that everyone else has one and understands it, and reading all the PDs and making sure they are aligned to what people are doing. This is where you uncover any discrepancies, whether real or perceived by your team. Plus it's an excellent opportunity to start the process of getting to know your team members.

I have found that many PDs are a bit boring and that simply 'jazzing up' the language that describes the same work can effectively motivate people. I have developed a template with a focus on inspiring the person, which includes setting targets and performance indicators which in turn makes exceeding expectations possible.

Overall, it's crucial for an IT manger or Team Leader to keep this basic function of clear job roles and expectations in check. Whether the measures are formal or informal, role administration is a key management process that each IT Manager and Team Leader is accountable for.

Special Projects

Each team will have its share of over-achievers (more on that later) and in order to help them, it is important to involve them in projects. Managers can establish a special projects list (often called Continual Service Improvement (CSI)) or, if the Projects team is a separate business unit, cultivate a relationship with them to connect high achievers. Then, when the Operations team are achieving all of their PD objectives, they can obtain experience doing projects that focus on advancing the current performance and creating internal transformation.

I have found mixing operations and project resources to be a very effective way of cross-skilling people and keeping them fresh and motivated. The grass can often seem to be greener on the other side ... Operations people are constantly in a reactive state, while those working in the Project area have to be proactive in order to be successful. Working out the priorities of the organisation and getting resource time is always a challenge, but it pays off. Involving Operations people in projects has on occasions delivered extraordinary results.

Early in my IT career, I learnt to juggle the need to support the lifeblood of our business and the challenges associated with growing it through project implementations. I made the decision that separating out these roles and giving people time away from Operations was the only way to for them to have a real experience of the project.

As an example: a customer decided to delay the go-live date for a major product to allow for additional auditing, and with the additional time, also decided to tack on additional project scope. Since I had delivered the project under budget, we had both money and time available, so it made sense to use them to deliver more benefits.

During the initial project, I had met a person in the Desktop Support team who was keen to get involved in project work. This was an opportunity to utilise their knowledge about the customer at the coalface. Their task was to document all IT requests that a customer may have – a daunting task that required some coaching and a lot of persistence to accomplish. But this opportunity to work on the project side meant they had a whole new perspective and could now make choices about their career and what most suited them.

Working through both the Operations and Project lenses enhances an employee's understanding of the differences between the roles. Giving the Operations people the opportunity to take an idea and implement it gives them the advantage of a new perspective. Seeing the big picture project through to the Operational state gives the Project people an appreciation of how to affect change. While too much switching back and forth between roles can be exhausting, some Operations people may find that 'the grass is greener' on the project side.

Making a difference in a person's life and seeing them grow is the most fulfilling part of being an IT Manager, particularly in an industry that has so much opportunity for career development.

Over-achievers

Typically, about 10% of the people on any given team are 'hungry'. They are working within a role to advance or stretch themselves. When I worked for someone else, either as an employee or a contractor, I figured that if I was going to spend my day working, I might as well enjoy it. My idea of enjoyment was to get the work I was there for out of the way and then get into the new and exciting stuff that I did not yet know.

When I meet a person like that, I like to take full advantage of their enthusiasm … as my Managers did with me. I sit down with them and ask them what they are good at, what they like doing, and where they think they want to go.

The great thing about IT is that there is so much to know, with new things and emerging technology all the time. The downside is that this vast and never-ending industry means that most only survive in what is known as a Tower of Knowledge, or as a Subject Matter Expert (SME). This specific and limited knowledge of course does not always easily or naturally work in favour of the organisation or the customer.

I have met and mentored a select group of excited and enthusiastic young up-and-coming employees over the years. Selfishly, I employed many of them as they were keen to experience all there was to offer, and I was eager to bring people like that onto my team. However, I did temper this by ensuring I maintained good customer relationships as the customer always came first. Often I would convince a person to stay even when times were tough, which is in itself a life lesson about overcoming situations that did not quite suit them.

Working for me wasn't always easy (but I was no slouch either!). I never asked a person to do a job that I had not previously done myself and I always showed them the shortcuts. Some were more pig-headed than others and wanted to do things the hard way. Even those people usually ultimately came around to my way of thinking (though only in desperation I am sure!). I have always let people set their own target timeframes unless they needed a challenge, in which case I would set it for them. Of course, it's not news that over-achievers always challenge themselves, and I have watched a lot suffer in silence and let some off the hook.

I believe that integrity is a big part of being part of a team, so I didn't take it lightly when, on a number of occasions, non-overachievers accused me of favoritism. You have probably heard complains like, 'Why does Jim get all the interesting work?'. I took this as an opportunity to convert this person by noting their interest and giving them a special project.

Soon enough, people realise 'special' does mean *special*, and they usually looked pretty ragged at the end of the project, yet at the same time they're satisfied with the outcome. For most of my business life, these very people have kept me motivated. I used to hear things like 'surround yourself with great people' and, in the early days, it certainly made life easier for me. Over time, I've come to feel good about being able to give high-achievers opportunities, and this has always been returned to me ten times over.

Like does attract like, and as a leader this can be a positive or a negative – it's entirely up to you! On one occasion, I remember interviewing a person for a role. I had never met anyone so enthusiastic before: they were willing to do anything – like they had 'ants in their pants'. This is a phrase I use frequently to describe the rare person who has that much energy that I could keep them occupied forever.

I believe that leading high-performing teams is a skill that can be learnt. If you can tap into all the excess energy available and organise the team so that everyone is working to capacity, getting a lot done becomes a lot easier. It does mean that as the leader, you do have to loosen the reigns. Harnessing the horsepower the first few times was challenging as I was a bit of a control freak. So to make sure we always arrived at exactly where I wanted to go, before each project commenced, I would paint a clear picture of what the endgame would look and feel like. I soon learned that if I channeled my nervous energy by having daily catch-ups with the over-achievers and listening and helping them solve issues and teaching them as much as I could, everything worked out.

Skills Profiling

Understanding the skillset of the people on your team, including what they like to do and what they want to learn, will allow for flexibility when there are resource challenges. It may also even help with succession planning.

Skills profiling also allows you to ensure that you have the right people within the team to undertake the responsibilities of each role and PDs within the team. Over time, many organisations end up with a significant mismatch between roles and the skills of those doing the role. A review conducted every 1–2 years by someone who is external to your organisation will provide valuable input that is not influenced by relationships that have formed within the team (for example, I can personally recommend checking out True Colours People Solutions at https://www.truecolourspeople-solutions.com.au). This, in turn, will help Managers discern how best to challenge and engage their team members in terms of their actual skillsets.

CHAPTER 2

Know Your Type:
Playing to the strength of others' perceptions

Over the years, I had a number of run-ins with personality awareness. The first was being called a 'b@#%#.' I was devastated, and I sulked for weeks (well, probably for days, but it felt like weeks to me!). I had obviously upset a client and maybe the early days of converting people from manual systems to automation with some integration was getting to me. Why didn't anybody just get computers? It all seemed pretty obvious to me!

To win my first big corporate job I had to sit a personality test. I thought this was interesting and had no clue what it was all about. It turned out to be a Myers-Briggs Type Indicator test, and for several hours I thought it was a weird experience. What was funny was the call I received from the person giving me the result. All that stands out to me now – aside from the fact that I got the job even though the problem-solving questions seemed so obvious I worried there must have been a trick to it I was missing – was that he called me 'an actress'. I was hugely offended by the term and suggested that he might like to call it 'adaptable' and leave it at that.

I must admit it took me a good 10 years to realise that the 'actress' personality trait was very effective when used appropriately. When I look back at how the 'actress' personality played out over my career, I can recognise a few instances of how this trait turned out to be a good thing. Putting on this persona allowed me to assume new techniques to deal with difficult situations.

Act willing to risk discussions with stakeholders

Let's face it: a bit of emotion when the 'customer experience' is at risk is warranted. I faced the dilemma brought on by a lack of empathy on a number of occasions where the customer wasn't considered; when IT really didn't know or understand the real impact and went ahead anyway. I couldn't always get my point across, and at times the customers suffered. I never have stopped stepping up to the plate on behalf of the customer.

Act unafraid to deliver repeat escalations

I recall reading somewhere that when you're not being taken seriously, it is important to change your delivery style. I don't think there was any mention at the time of the technique one could use to get results (oh, the politics – but that is a whole different book!). Maybe it was Tony Robbins who said, 'repetition is the mother of all skill' and Winston Churchill who said, 'Never, never, never give up'.

Again, the actress in me learnt to change my delivery as it can achieve a different result!

Act in ways that add value

I've always hated hearing 'you're just a contractor' because I know I don't act like one. So when I heard this, I realised that

I was threatening the person's role and needed to find an alternative approach so they felt comfortable and not intimidated by me. What I found worked was if I delivered a piece of work and gave it to them so they could use it if they wanted – everyone likes freebies! Be a giver not a taker – always add value.

Act as if you know your role when necessary

This one's a bit tricky. I never kidded myself that I was doing a job that someone did not want to do or could not do. Where I could, I tried to impart and share knowledge; however, sometimes 'the boss is the boss' and you have to agree with people and make the best of it.

The times I struggled most to accept 'the chain of command' were when my integrity was on the line and my values were not consistent with the leaders' decision-making. I learnt to 'leave my ego at the door' and decide if what I signed up for was achievable regardless of the leadership.

Act reasonable

I have always been a person who likes to tackle things head on, but I have learnt that this is relative to the amount of time you have available. If time is scarce, then this approach and its ensuing side journey may not be a good way to spend it. I have been known to dig in my heels and go for the long haul to sort out the source, or root cause, of a problem, and I've learnt that]in some cases, it is a person.

Dealing with the systemic people issues at an organisational level has sometimes felt like being 'superwoman'. Ultimately, you think you're saving the world, but it can come at a personal cost. Being prepared for "what doesn't kill you makes you stronger" is all part of understanding when to go from A to B or via C,D,E,F to get to a better destination – like G.

Ultimately, knowing myself and being authentic has been one of the biggest challenges within my career. I have had some supporting nicknames in the industry which illustrate just how my personality plays out in my work life:

- *Perfumed Steamroller* – I do like my perfumes and I am pretty tough.
- *Madame Lash* – I got a whip and bottle of gin as a Kris Kringle present one year. I used both during that project! (I also met a girl who ran an IT business along the way, and her business was called Julia's Whip so I wasn't alone.)
- *Man hater* – Whenever I heard this I knew it was only gender bias talking. It wasn't true, and I knew I could get references to say this was definitely untrue.
- *Bully* – This one struck a nerve. Ever since the school playground when I found myself defending the innocent against such beasts, I realised that the person was referring to themselves. If I caught a hint of this in my own workplace persona, I'd be sure it was attended to and resolved, as there is nothing worse than a person feeling belittled.

Listening to how people talk about you can provide useful feedback. Even when you disagree, paying attention to what upsets you in their assessment can reflect your own values back to you. And when they're praising you, that's always great to hear too!

I started reading about personalities back in the mid-nineties, and the first book I tackled was *Personality Plus: How to Understand Others by Understanding Yourself* by Florence Littauer. As you may have also found, when you start reading a book about a topic, you spend most of it thinking about all the people you know that it applies to … until the big moment comes when you realise that you are a mix of the personality type that you most dislike in others.

I took this as an opportunity to make some personal adjustments. The first thing I had to accept was the fact that I took my work more seriously than most and that I had a melancholy side that really was 'not fit for human consumption'. I also had to accept that the other personalities out there made up the workplace, too, and rather than avoiding them I'd need to start to work at bringing out the best in each type. I used this thinking a lot over the years both in managing for a better fit of person to each role and in reaching towards a better understanding of myself.

I have read many books about people and human behavior over the years, and have found that it is important to understand this subject with interest in order get to know yourself better and be more authentic. Some Managers naturally have leadership skills; however, many need to learn how to lead people by understanding people and themselves better. I have worked for a number of wonderful leaders who knew just how to motivate and support me. It had an incredible impact on what I was prepared to do and what I ended up achieving. I continue to learn, grow and be human.

CHAPTER 3

Go and Observe:
Witness how others view your technology

OPPORTUNITY OF A LIFETIME: Starting with a concrete floor, build a Contact Centre and then open for business!

You cannot assume anything about the way data is created unless you watch the behavior of the people creating it. What is even more astounding is what drives human behavior when they interact with a system. With every new project, I go and observe so I don't have to assume anything when I analyse the data. I can then see the correlation between the data quality and human behavior and then set about resolving the root cause – human behavior.

I once got a call from a person I had worked for who had moved on to build a startup business. They wanted a Project Manager (PM), and there was voice work involved – in other words, telephones. I had nailed the data (computer) work, so diving into voice work was such a joy. They offered to pay for training, which, as a contractor, was unheard of. I went on the training, and when I realised that a PABX (telephone switch) was a Unix box, I felt like I had landed in heaven.

With great gusto I arrived on the construction site after the training. The sound of my heels on the concrete caused the workmen to stop working and start whispering. I hadn't realised that having a woman on a construction site was such as distraction. I had to spend time building a working relationship with the construction team as I would be totally dependent on them completing the connectivity later on in the project.

The first site meeting to determine the layout of the equipment in the Computer Room or mini Data Centre turned into a rather nasty event. Someone got fired. My practical approach of getting a tape measure and confirming the size of each piece of equipment upset the Project Manager from the parent company, who preferred the 'fly by the seat of your pants' approach.

That left one less person with an opinion. So now I was totally in charge and everyone was clear on where their equipment was to go. It was at this point that I rang my mother and asked why everyone was treating me like I was not supposed to be in charge? But she responded by simply reassuring me, saying, 'Don't worry. There really is no difference between men and women'. This seemed to fit with my paradigm so I put it behind me and took charge.

This was a life-changing project for many reasons. Firstly, I lead the build of the Data Centre from the floor plan to completion, with multiple service providers. I engaged the service provider executives very early on and laid out the project plan and timeline to ensure buy-in, asking their permission to call them personally if any issues arose. Having many service providers involved it is key to reducing the risk of delays and escalations, and it underpins a healthy long-term relationship. Getting approval from the top down helps remove resource issues that may emerge during the delivery of a project.

Secondly, I was able to sit with the business users, get hands on, and ask them what they wanted and how they expected the technology to work. We focused a lot on the 'look and feel', as it was clear that we saw everything through completely different lenses. I got a very clear perspective on how they wanted the technology to operate, and I documented these requirements. I then set about building a prototype and asked managers, team leaders, and analysts to test it and provide feedback. This wasn't an easy process; however, I wanted to spare us any disappointments in the future.

Thirdly, I finished the project with all of the technology operational and ready to go – ahead of the business units. This was my plan all along, just to see if I could be first. Yes, I am competitive when it comes to challenging myself. I had a two-hundred-seat call centre operational a month in advance of opening the doors, and this gave me breathing space to check and double check that all the technology was fully tested and functional and that it met the needs of the business.

Lastly, I got a standing ovation for the first time in my life and a huge bunch of flowers presented to me by the organisation's CEO. This became an anchor for success, underlining for me the concept that it is possible to deliver beyond what people expect.

I had the opportunity to observe that management team, established by their CEO, and to see how they set up their divisions. This gave me some amazing insights into different management styles and personalities. The Manager for the Contact Centre who was responsible for onboarding two hundred people shared many of her thoughts on leadership, which I found to be very valuable in later projects.

She taught me:

- Onboard people early so they have plenty of time to settle in.
- Be flexible at the team leader layer and it will reap rewards in terms of flexible staff.
- Be very clear with your directions: be firm, be specific, and be confident.
- Select people with the right attitude.
- Match the team leader to the team members and line of business as this is critical to success.
- Don't short-cut training – ever, or it will come back to bite you later on.

After establishing the Help Desk I handed the project over to an Operations Manager, and then I was on my way to the next challenge.

CHAPTER 4

Right People in the Right Teams:
How teams can stay abreast of change

One of the key characteristics you look for within a person is their ability to communicate. A common comment I get from IT people is: 'I don't have time to communicate, when I am too busy trying to fix the problem'. Most poor customer service stems from a lack of willingness to communicate, and for most people, that really means they need to overcommunicate. I lead by example and seek to show people the many different ways to communicate, and how good communication creates trust and integrity.

I was introduced to the concept of organisational change management very early on and participated in a significant outsourcing project where each person was given a copy of *Who Moved My Cheese* – Ken Blanchard's classic motivational book about change management. When embarking on major change, it doesn't take long to realise that there are always people who go back to the same place – even, as in Blanchard's example, if there is no food and they may die. It's amazing what lengths a person will go to just to avoid change!

My motto is, if there is doubt about the future, take the bull by the horns and move on! It is better to be the dumper than the dumpee.

Once change is set in motion – the cheese has moved, and the team is in the boat and is sailing to the new world – I always look around at the team and consider who is really in the boat, oars in the water and rowing. Over the years what I have confirmed is:

- 10% are in the boat, oars in the water, rowing, and focused on the finish line.
- 30% are in the boat, oars in the water and rowing.
- 30% are in the boat and playing with the oars.
- 30% are over the side struggling to hang on.

Identifying who is in which category really helps me understand how the change is affecting the team. Those who see change as an opportunity can be more involved and help drive that change. The next group will be motivated by those who see the opportunity, and the group after that will be watching and waiting to see if the boat is really sailing. Those who resist the change will tend to take most of the time, and this can be the category that forces a Manager to make tough decisions about which team members would be better off moving on to other opportunities. Don't get me wrong: some people can be saved, and I have always worked hard to convert people and help them to become engaged. Others just need to cut their losses and find a new place of work, either within or outside the company.

During my career I have helped many people find new roles and sometimes even a new career. This has been a very satisfying part of being involved in change programs, although it is not a popular or easy one. As I have placed myself in the situation of change in moving between projects and companies, I now take the time to explain to people who struggle how I have dealt with change. When I have shared that this is a skill you can learn, many people relax and can work through it. Some take it as an opportunity to make more significant change (work, life, health), and I make a point of being there to support them through these transitions.

When the opportunity to mentor a person landed in my lap, or I offered my support when I saw a person suffering, almost every time it has resulted in a positive outcome. In some cases I have seen people go on to do extraordinary things. I have never been short of confidence, so the opportunity to help a person with low self-belief by sharing some of the tools I have used to support myself along the way has led to the development of some amazing friendships. When I have gone through tough times, these are the people who have been there to support me and help me get my confidence back again.

During one of these times of change, I was introduced to the role of a headhunter: an external person focused on establishing a management team with the necessary skills and capability required to lead the team into the future. I was exposed to how successful targeted talent selection can be. I prepared all the position descriptions and worked closely with the headhunter to impart my sense of the type of person that would be most suitable for each role.

The results were nothing short of extraordinary, and this shifted my paradigm forever. I developed a long-term relationship with this headhunter and relied on their services for many later projects.

Getting people with the right attitude to join your organisation is like creating a parallel universe. The shift in culture can be almost immediate. It's hard to tell people what 'great' looks like, so showing them is by far the quickest way to create a shift in mindset. When the new starts to out-weigh the old and you have turned the corner, there is no going back. I estimate it takes 90 days to establish a new way of doing things, and I use this estimate as a planning and goal-setting tool. You'd be surprised what you can achieve in 90 days!

CHAPTER 5

Change Something to Create Progress:
The danger of out-of-touch Managers

As soon as I have the feeling that a person is not the right person for the job, I have nearly always proven to have been right. It can be disappointing or uncomfortable, but never leave this decision too long, or everyone suffers. Every time I have left someone in a role they weren't suited for, I have always looked back and wished I had done something sooner. But when I do make these challenging calls, I have been driven by the health of the team and a feeling of responsibility to make the tough decisions so the team is the best it can be. I live according to the philosophy if you don't change something, nothing changes.

On the first day at a new project where I was engaged by a board member, I met with the Helpdesk and IT Projects Manager. They could not seem to get the reports out that management needed. They said that the system couldn't manage the reporting workload or the staff were not using the system properly. Over the years, I have worked out that if an operational manger does not understand the system their team uses to track and manage the team workload, it is a big red flag suggesting that something isn't right. On top of that, hearing a Manager blaming the team never really sits well with me.

At this point, I always request to attend the next team meeting, and if a team meeting does not already exist, this is another red flag for me. In this case, a team meeting was held weekly. During the first team meeting for this project, though, I noticed that the team were very quiet and not really contributing to the discussion. This type of disconnect between the team and its managers is always a symptom of a bigger problem.

Where there are no daily or weekly team meetings, then the manager is not managing; rather they are flying by the seat of their pants. In every organisation I have ever worked in, the very first thing I do is establish a daily meeting. The challenge as a Manager is to make these worthwhile and no longer than 15 minutes, and to get everyone contributing to (or at least enjoying) them.

I have found that the key is to use this time to share something from the executive with the team or have a guest join the meetings for an update. That way, people will show up for the meeting just so they don't miss anything rather than seeing it as an inconvenience. If you are not inspiring your team daily, you may be in the wrong job! It is important to keep in mind that everyone learns in a different way and at a different rate. As a Manager, you must deliver your messages and communication in different ways and remember that you are accountable for your team getting it!

To make progress on this project, I requested that the Managers be re-deployed to other tasks while I took over managing the Helpdesk and Desktop Support in the interim. These physical changes are sometimes necessary to make it clear that change is happening. I have noticed that teams quickly work out the credibility of their Manager. If the Manager doesn't have the team's respect, and if they can't make serious adjustments to regain their credibility, then they have to go. Coaching a Manager can work, but I rarely see long-term change happen without significantly changing the team mix.

In this case, I hit the 'reset button' with the team. The advantage to coming in fresh to a problematic situation is that I can question everything, change and test it with the team, and agree if it is an improvement. I started with a team session to determine:

- What are our personal and team goals?
- How are we measured?
- Do we have the skills and people in the right roles?
- Are we using the system the same way?
- What are our requirements of the system?
- Does the system meet our requirements?
- What are the obstacles we face?

For the next 30 days, following on from a meeting like that, I kept the focus on the team and how well they worked together. Interesting enough, once the Managers were gone, the team stepped up to the plate. The Managers never came back to their former positions. This was the shortest project ever. The senior team member walked into my office after a few weeks and said they wanted a crack at the job. They had the support of the team, so I moved out and they moved into the Manager's office and the project was completed.

CHAPTER 6

Personalities Influence Projects:
How to juggle daily work and special projects

Involving those people responsible for daily operations in a project is challenging but critical for success.

With the rapid changes in technology and ever-increasing expectations, it is often necessary for Operations people to juggle both operations and projects. I observed that most people found this to be a huge challenge, possibly beyond their abilities. Many worried they could not successfully juggle between operations support and projects.

I don't assume that Operations Managers and Team Leaders know how to lead and manage resources to deliver both operational activities and project deliverables. I get resources assigned to the project for set weekly times to ensure that there is no slippage or miscommunication regarding what is expected. Some people in fact can juggle activities and meet deadlines, and this is always a nice surprise when it happens, but it is never my expectation.

Taking this one step further, when the operational resources find the project work to be interesting and fun, they can become the best champions for the project. They can help dispel any friction or resistance to the change brought about by technology transformation by leveraging their relationships on both sides of the fence.

Operations can be a very different beast requiring different skills than those required for a project. Where Operations is mostly reactive to issues raised by customers and based on customer priorities, project work is mostly pro-active with pre-determined commitments.

Planning a project and identifying those people who will need to be involved, invariably leads to the identification of Subject Matter Experts (SMEs) who work in Operations. I always produce a project plan, resource plan, and schedule in draft form with an estimate of the hours per week required for each role to meet the project deliverables. I walk through the plans and schedule with the Managers and Team Leaders so they have an opportunity to review the draft documents and provide their input.

I often uncover extreme variations in the capabilities of Managers and Team Leaders (along with SMEs performing crucial operational tasks which result in single points of failure). I escalate these concerns to the project executive so they are aware of the gaps in capability and single points of failure in order to support the Manager or Team Leader in resolving them. It is crucial that all the resource issues are uncovered and resolved with an agreed-upon weekly commitment in terms of their resources before the project starts.

I have watched Operations teams juggle the day-to-day operational activities with project deliverables and miss deadlines. This of course has a negative impact on the project and can be frustrating for everyone involved. Some of the reasons why Operations teams struggle include: imbalances in workload and resources, lack of time management skills, lack of experience in prioritising, or the challenge of having to work in two different hemispheres of the brain, both reactive and proactive.

I devised some questions to help define the different types of people that can show up in operational teams and I use these to guide discussions with Managers and Team Leaders. Where operational people are joining the project team, it is important to know what I might be in for in terms of people challenges. I use language that helps lighten up what can be a difficult discussion when asking Managers and Team Leaders to evaluate their team:

1. *Who likes feeding from the queue?* There are people who work best when they are provided with work, and in the order that it needs to be done. Getting these people to change their style, though, can be nearly impossible, so not being aware of them can have an impact and be a risk to the project.

2. *Who are the adrenalin junkies?* Some people like the pressure that comes with critical issues and find it too boring to work on projects. At times they have tried to convince me that they need a break from the pressure, however I have found it takes up to three months for them to come down from the high and be productive. I am happy to accommodate that rehabilitation, as long as they are not a resource with deliverables on the critical path.

3. *Who can't meet deliverables and dates?* This happens more than I would like to admit and is a huge risk to any project. The difficultly here is that Managers or Team Leaders don't address this as part of operations, and the person is unprepared for the consequences when it happens on a project.

4. *Who has a BO personality?* A person who continually puts people off them – either intentionally or

unintentionally – is what I call a BO personality. I know this sounds harsh, but using language that people are familiar with can make it easier to discuss. These people simply stink, and no one wants to be around them. Sometimes they can respond positively to a change in work or a shift onto a new team with positive leadership. But it's always best to trial this beast before committing to any permanent arrangement.

5. *Who is easily bored and wants a challenge?* I am wary of this type of person unless they have a history of delivering and meeting/exceeding expectations. The challenges that come with major programs test the most experienced with little wiggle room for failure, so it is crucial to make sure this type of person is not running from a previous history of failure.

6. *Who is a handful?* What one Manager or Team Leader sees as a handful may in fact with a rough diamond. People who rock the boat and contest the status quo in operations can often be better suited to project work. They can channel all their energy into creating 'a new world' rather than being held back by the limitations of 'the way it has always been done'.

CHAPTER 7

All or Nothing:
Top-down training builds consistent teams

The last piece of the puzzle in delivering transformation within any orgnisation is training. I have attended a lot of training sessions over the years and found many of them to be ineffective. I decided to explore different methods of getting people to understand concepts and then have them apply it themselves in their work role.

This may sound old-fashioned, but I don't conduct training with Operations people unless their Manager or Team Leader attends every session. I have experienced some terrible training sessions where I have asked trainees to leave as they seem incapable of participating without focusing on the negative or refusing to change.

I have always been passionate about training and firmly believe that, after all the hard work and challenges, project success hinges on the training. There is an art to getting into the heads of those being trained and working out how to 'get the lights to go on'. I have learnt about human conditioning from some of the best minds and have discovered the benefits of teaching a new behavior via the process of association.

Importantly, I believe that understanding human behavior creates quality data.

In all the training sessions that I have conducted, I have found that it is essential to build a relationship among the people, the process, the technology, the partners, and the projects to create change. Being interactive, drawing on a whiteboard, getting input and discussing each area of change that makes up a successful transformation is necessary to get the trainees to invest in the training.

I always commence a training session with the problems to solve and ensure that these are consistent with the participants' perspective. Having an agreed-upon starting position creates a sense of curiosity, and the appropriate opening to explaining the journey that the project has been on.

Showing people the whole picture and then drilling down into their world means that the trainer must have operational experience and must be able to answer questions. I always have another person accompanying me to write down all the questions asked and all the answers I provided during the training session. Crucially, when I could not give someone an answer they were satisfied with, I would take time to reply in writing.

The questions and answers that come from training must be shared with everyone and be converted into knowledge articles – that is, a written reference. It is crucial that whatever is raised in training must be addressed to give the project credibility, even as the timeline draws to a close.

It should also be a requirement for all participants to assess and rate the training quality before leaving the training session. Reviewing all the feedback in the initial sessions means that you can adapt and make changes to the training if the scores are low or the comments indicate it is not hitting the target that the training was meant to achieve.

In addition, many Managers and Team Leaders don't get to work very closely with their team members, particularly if they are highly technical, don't share the same technical background, are not co-located, and/or they don't socialise with their team members outside of work. In this case, training can be an opportunity for Managers to get to know their people and the way they behave outside of the daily work environment.

Over the years, I have built various simulation games that I include in the training to make it a bit more hands on for participants. This has helped to lighten what can at times be a dry subject. I plan to release these resources in the form of a mobile application sometime in the future so they can be shared and used.

As a final note, I always measure attendance to my training sessions and have a rule that everyone must complete the training – no exceptions. You may be surprised to know that there are people out there who make it their life's mission to avoid training! We always schedule in make-up sessions at the end of the planned training period to accommodate those people who were sick, on holidays, or away from work for any reason. There is also a group that may have had to attend to operational issues that occurred on the training days. I provide a report to the executives listing everyone's name, and in the rare case where we did not get 100% attendance, the names of those who did not attend the session.

There is a direct correlation between training attendance and transformation success.

CHAPTER 8

All Data is Man-made:
The importance of measurability

Throughout my career, having a focus on the analytics (data and reporting) has always paid off. I wouldn't say that it was easy, that I didn't get resistance, or that it happened quickly; however, embedding an appreciation of analytics into the organisational culture is a great foundation for any operation. To be able to demonstrate a commitment to measuring and improving performance is what I consider to be good governance. One of the numerous benefits of this process is instilling confidence in and gaining trust from the executive and the customers.

In the more complex transformation projects I have delivered, especially where people are not co-located, there is an added burden on the data as it starts to mean different things to different people even if their job is the same. This puts an onus on the executive team to be cohesive, and to strive to drive common goals with one unified culture.

It starts with one management structure across multiple locations, but in practice, most people see their Team Leader or Manager as the management structure. It requires a focus on communicating a broader set of objectives, not just what is visible day to day. In addition, when there are vendors involved, there is an even greater challenge.

I believe the way to getting superior quality data is by having a commitment to understanding the people and how they create it. This is definitely a team sport, hence, it must become embedded into the culture of an organisation and span all levels of management, all vendors and across all capabilities.

In most cases, the common thread and focus is the technology that is used and the way in which it is used. If there are multiple technologies in play, then this again adds more complexity. I focus on reporting and feeding the results back to the teams and drawing the connection between the creation of the data and how it is reported. This is a continual process of validation – daily, weekly, monthly, and quarterly – to ensure that there is confidence in the reporting structure and that the KPIs in place to measure performance are true and correct.

The 4PT Framework:
PROCESS

CHAPTER 9

Working in Unison:
Service Integration is a team sport

Like all operations and businesses, IT has its own unique set of processes, or at least that's what I originally thought. However, as I progressed within the field, what I observed was not a consistent sense of how things worked or should work. Instead, there seemed to be a disconnect between identifying a process and the very people who would play a role in bringing that process to life.

I was already well-versed in relation to how process can and should work when I launched myself into IT. My experiences in accounting and payroll had given me a strong sense of how key processes played out across various industries. In addition, my strong understanding of programming on mainframes and data centre operations had shown me how a process works from the inside out. Yet, I found myself like 'a fish out of water'; expecting all the other IT people would know what a process was as well.

Instead, it looked to me as though many IT people operated as if the things that happened in their work environments were all random events, whereas I understood that inputs, processes, and outputs were all linked and interconnected, and not at all random. I often thought about the common phrase 'garbage in, garbage out' and recognised that there were upstream and downstream implications for everything that happened in IT.

The concept that a person did not question a process as the possible cause of the problem was foreign to me since, by then, it was second nature to me to review the process straightaway. So, when I built the technology for a business processing contact centre, I made sure that a significant effort went into developing repeatable processes.

It took me quite a while to accept that processes are created by a small percentage of people involved in the business while others, who aren't aware of this initial development, tend to 'fly by the seat of their pants', assuming that's just how things worked. Eventually, I accepted that it was my calling in life to implement process wherever I worked.

When ITIL (Information Technology Infrastructure Library) came along, providing a common vocabulary and resource, I was relieved to have this benchmark to reference. No more: 'Because Christine McNamara said so'! The ITIL Framework established formal and standard processes across IT in the form of a set of books and training courses. These books incorporated process diagrams to describe how common activities, such as incident resolution, could be executed in a consistent manner. These process diagrams could be adjusted to align with an organisation's approach and then be configured into a technology tool to further enhance standard practices.

However, while ITIL did provide a framework and common language that was helpful for training and documentation purposes, the books didn't always address the relationship between the process and the people – the behavioral aspect. To bridge that gap between the process itself and the people who make the process work, I created a number of other processes which I have used repeatedly with a great deal of success.

The following table showcases a few examples of my processes:

Where is the Redbook?
A Redbook is simply a folder that is easily located and is accessible to the Service Desk or any team delivering services. Previously, it was a printed copy of the key documents in an actual red folder (I know, how old fashioned!). Nowadays, a shared digital resource is a viable alternative, as long as team members can each access the same folder, rather than local and potentially outdated versions.
Let's face it: if a team (and not just the Service Desk) cannot manage to keep a folder updated and accessible, do you really think they will be able to keep knowledge easily referenced by the whole team for a consistent customer experience?
The key items in the folder should include the organisational structure, how to answer the phone, important phone numbers, customer initiation pack (or things you need to know when dealing with customers), and the answers to the top ten customer issues.
It's a bit like giving a child an egg to mind for the day. If the egg is the customer, and the child comes home with a broken egg, then the customer experience is obviously broken. It's that black and white!
Customers respect consistency, so IT people can quickly gain credibility by simply answering the phone clearly and

in the same manner every time. This small consistency was actually fairly rare in my experience, and I would always be particular about this point. There is a skill involved in answering the phone in a way that makes the customer feel valued.

Believe it or not, many people do not answer the phone properly by ending the greeting with their name, pronounced clearly, in an up-tone, after taking a breath. This gives the customer the opportunity to process the person's name and speak first.

Realistically, if you work in IT, then whoever is calling isn't phoning to see how your health is. They have a technical issue, and they believe you can solve it. Initiating the conversation by truly wanting to be of assistance will almost always start things off on the right note.

Here's an example. If the phone rings and I'm answering, I will say, 'Welcome to the IT Service Desk. This is Christine'. Then stop.

Hopefully, the customer replies, 'Hi, this is Helen', and then goes on to tell you what she needs.

Starting with the basics can help customers see your team as people who not only provide a service but also care about your customer experience as well. That is a great baseline from which to develop your processes.

Consistency is one of the keys to a great customer experience. To achieve it, each team needs to find a way to share information and resources to ensure everyone gives the same right answer, no matter who takes the call.

To test this with your team, put them all in a room and write a common customer problem on the board. Get them to write down exactly how they would respond. It may feel confrontational, but if everyone's answers are all the same, that's great. If not, then there is work to be done.

I often use my daily stand-up meetings to go over basic processes to ensure they are at the top of my team's minds or the focus of the day. If I am not focused on the customer, then the team isn't likely to be either.

Who is in the Hot Seat?

I created an empty chair at the Service Desk which I called the Hot Seat. The idea behind this was for it to be filled by a member of IT (not from the Service Desk) for four hours on rotation (weekly or monthly, depending).

This four-hour IT shift is used to:

- test the onboarding processes of a new person to the Service Desk (which can be a high turnover area).
- give technical people adequate time to document issues and responses. (I recommend each person documents between ten to twenty queries and fixes during that four hours to improve the ratio of 'fix-on-first contact' stats.)
- offer technical people a new or renewed appreciation of being on the frontline and answering the phone in a professional manner.

Some other benefits include:

- relationship-building opportunities between IT and the Service Desk, when they are working together and have 'the shoe on the other foot'.
- technical team mates recognise the value in knowledge sharing through cross-training with the Service Desk team.

- the techos feel satisfied and have renewed confidence that they can answer almost any question as a result of the knowledge they have shared and acquired.
- a better understanding of such basics as answering the phone in a polite manner, just in case the customer does call them directly!

Of course, it goes without saying that the first person in the Hot Seat should be the CTO or CIO – that is, the most senior IT person, if not the CEO! If the CEO, CTO or CIO spends four hours in the Hot Seat, then there are no excuses for the rest of the team members not to participate.

One team

Employees, contractors and vendors are part of one team.

I have never understood why contractors or vendors are excluded from the overall employee experience. It seems to me that if they are paid more, then they should be expected to know more and, likewise, they should help more.

Throughout my time in IT, the most meaningful compliment I've received when someone finds out that I am a contractor or consultant is also one of the most common remarks I hear: 'Really? I thought you were an employee!' It always makes me smile.

Whenever vendors and contractors are treated differently from the employees, problems can arise. The customer doesn't know the difference but, instead, looks for one team – where everyone is working together to fix their problem.

Sit down when the music stops

If you build a culture of change, then people develop the necessary skills to change.

It all starts with a person's desk and what happens when you ask them to move.

We know that IT attracts a large percentage of introverts. This attitude may have suited the back-office nature of IT in the 80s and 90s. However, things have changed since then, and while introverts may still gravitate to an IT role, an increased level of engagement within the team is now required.

There are lots of advantages to moving people around, including:

- People get to know each other better.
- People working on similar tasks or projects often benefit from being co-located (or at least cloud-located).
- Everyone gets to share 'the window seat' (if they are well-located).
- The Manager gets to experience each person at close range. (Yes, I do advocate for the Manager to sit with the rest of the team, even if there is a separate office available, or to take advantage of technology to co-work, like using Skype with the video on.)

Let's simulate it

Humans are funny creatures with notoriously poor communication skills; even when we are all speaking English, we can hear different things.

I am a big fan of simulating processes, and I've had a lot of fun with executive simulations, in particular. I once asked a group of managers to run through a major incident process, and the simulation made it quite clear – much to their embarrassment and amusement – that the processes they were asking their staff to follow were processes that they themselves certainly couldn't complete perfectly.

I have often used simulations as a method to continually train people, and from this experience, I've developed a number of simulation games.

The Service Desk is the centre of the Universe

The fact that the Service Desk is the center of the IT Universe is a surprise to most people.

If the frontline people in IT are not the most important, then who is? We all know if your business is not managing your customers well, then you are in trouble.

When the Service Desk team members know everything that is going on, where it is, and how to get there, there are numerous benefits, from fewer customer escalations to lower operation costs. In this way, when a Service Desk member requires an explanation from a technical person, documentation of that issue and its fix is key, so it is available for the rest of the team to reference for themselves.

Getting this right buys lots of credits 'when the chips are down' and the IT systems go AWOL.

Operationalise the contract

There's an old saying that if you are referring to the contract, then you are in trouble. It's usually a sign that something isn't working properly.

Every contract must be converted from a business agreement into operations that meet its goals. My approach has been to sit down with my clients and walk through every service level and discuss what it is trying to achieve. Then, we agree upon the mapping and integration of the data that will drive the reporting. This is an essential stage at the beginning, because, generally speaking, once data is already being created, it can be a challenge to go back and start again.

If there is money involved, then you cannot afford to have people improvising with the process or the data. Over the term of a contract, this could lead to enormous misalignment of operations, which is a wasted effort spent on fixing reporting rather than addressing the root cause, which is the process and the resulting data.

There is no shortcut to this process, and simulating the way every service level is measured will reduce the risk of conflict in the future.

Who is managing the customer?

For some organisations, the idea of managing the customer does not seem to be much of a problem. In this situation, customers are in frequent contact with the team, and if the culture of that organisation is a customer-focused one, then who manages the customer does not come into question; the customer has easy access to the team, who all prioritise the customer's needs.

In many organisations where the IT department is not well-regarded, it is less likely to be so defined whose job it is to work with the customers directly. It is imperative to establish who is directly accountable, and to then identify all those responsible and be clear about what is expected from them and when.

I have found, over the years, that the strongest and most patient people are the people who should be facing the customer. This is as much a sales role as it is a delivery role. I was lucky to learn about the value of a strong and trusted relationship with customers from some of the best account managers.

When a major gap exists between customer expectations and what the IT team is delivering, it is time to put myself in the customer's shoes to find out exactly where the problem is. More often than not, issues co-exist at all levels of the organisation and across different towers of knowledge and specialisation. Capturing all the data, verifying its accuracy, and developing a plan to fix the weaknesses has always been my starting position.

Creating a governance structure around the customer and working closely with them to agree upon touch-points (that is, when the customer gets into contact with the team), priorities, escalation paths, and reporting has always been met with open arms. This alignment must then be followed by the delivery, in line with the process and expectations laid out. It can take months to shift old experiences and attitudes, but it is well worth staying the distance to arrive at a place where the customer feels valued.

Theory of Constraints

Processes always include constraints, which can help keep us all on our toes. By focusing on finding the bottlenecks – that is, where the processes get jammed up and things stop flowing so smoothly – we can observe where a change can be implemented to improve efficiency levels (refer to the book titled *The Goal: A Process of Ongoing Improvement* by Eliyahu Goldratt). I always assumed this was what a process owner did until I realised that not everyone understands the Theory of Constraints.

Essentially, service level attainment is the goal – whether these are agreements or objectives we want to deliver. There is no shortcut to understanding each of the steps in a process and being familiar with the throughput (that is, the amount of material, information, or items moving through a process), its cost, and the resources required.

When I first learned about the concept of 'Lean' I was pleased to have a logical set of steps that could lead to a better understanding of efficiency. I also realised in that same moment that what I have built is Lean IT.

SMO

Over the years, I have built a number of Service Management Offices (SMOs) and, in some cases, I've left with a few regrets.

In the early ITIL days, I was fortunate to get the opportunity to work alongside an ITIL guru who shared with me the basis for Process Management, and the roles and responsibilities involved. I built the first SMO wrapped around an IT Service Desk.

This was a hugely successful project for that organisation, and in subsequent projects, I figured I had found the answer to implementing ITIL and taking it from a theoretical framework into the real world.

Sadly, over the years, the combined SMO and Service Desk often created a monster. Sometimes, Process Owners were given roles without the necessary operational experience, customer focus, or training, and were paid significantly higher than other staff, without the skills required to do the job well or to justify the increased compensation. I had to admit that the days when those who moved into service management were the most customer-focused technical people was not the case anymore.

After building six SMOs over twelve years (both within large organisations and for service providers), I believe the most significant skill required for a Service Management Office to be successful is the ability of the SMO to influence the operation and the overall delivery of the customer experience. The placement of the SMO within the organisational structure, its mandate, the skill of the process managers and the culture are also critical success factors.

In summary, Service Management has now combined with Service Integration and become Service Integration and Management (SIAM). SIAM is a team sport encompassing internal and external people (known as suppliers of the service). If the basics of managing the team are not in place, then it is only a matter of time before the cracks and silos form, separating groups from one another. This in turn impedes knowledge sharing, as well as having a negative impact on service delivery and ultimately the customer experience.

CHAPTER 10

The Short Answer is Not Always the Best One:
Getting buy-in for change

Simply providing the right answer or demonstrating all the skill in the world won't get you executive buy-in. It's when the evidence, that is the data, is presented along with an analysis of what it means that you are able to garner executive interest. You get buy-in when the data and analysis supports the anecdotal knowledge. That is how a baseline is formed to open the door for discussing transformation.

But any lower than the Executive level, the data often is sometimes seen as threatening because it exposes the weaknesses of the operation. Building a platform that enables executives to see gaps in capability has revolutionised my consulting business by helping everyone to agree on where to focus.

There is no shortcut for experience. In my first week on one job, I became aware that many of the IT Management team, along with other IT team members, doubted my ability to resolve the serious technical issues that were affecting their day-to-day business operations.

The network was 'bouncing' during the day and people were either having trouble logging in or their login session was unreliable, which meant they got booted out and had to log in again. Naturally, this made for many unhappy IT customers.

In passing, I said to the IT Management team that these symptoms were most likely a result of the cable runs being too long. I knew that the maximum length for RG58 Ethernet network cable was 183 metres, with a limit of between twenty to thirty access points or workstations, and I suspected these were much longer, given the way the network was acting. Of course, environmental factors were likely playing a part, but since this was a bank, I expected they would be in shipshape condition. I suggested they rent a Time-domain Reflectometer (TDR), which would allow me to do the testing, but they dismissed this suggestion as another crazy idea.

The next thing I knew, Management had paid a consultant to come in and test the cable lengths. To me, this seemed like a crazy idea. I wasn't a bit surprised when the consultant found the cable runs were too long, at 250m. I could only laugh, because I had all the qualifications necessary to operate a TDR, had they agreed with my recommendation to rent one. For a quarter of the cost, I could have done myself what they paid the additional consultant to do. If only they had asked me (or listened to my suggestion), they could have saved themselves a lot of money.

Over the next few months, I upgraded the servers and expanded the networks – all the while continuing my original task of resolving customer issues that had been plaguing them for ages. I continued to perform with all eyes on me waiting for me to fail. But no such luck for my doubters! After five years of experience, getting my hands dirty on every piece of equipment and software available, along with my determination to never be conquered by a piece of code, and with my good grounding in testing, I knew I could just keep changing and re-testing until it eventually worked.

During my time with this company, they were relocating, and we had to move the Data Centre. I had the opportunity to use all my skills in cabling and patching and to learn new technology at lightening pace. As usual, all it took was to Read the Manual (or as we techos say for short: RTFM!).

In those early days, I developed a few opinions about mixing and matching technology. For the most part, nobody really knew if anything would work until it was tried. One of the conclusions that I came to was that Operating System programmers have a lot to answer for; I would often spend many hours figuring out how to install the Operating System on hardware by mostly stepping through error after error, reading manuals and making phone calls to get everything working.

I learnt some key rules during that time which have helped me stay sane when it comes to technology, including:

- All the testing in the world sometimes still isn't enough, and you need a Plan B.
- You can do the same thing over and over, and sometimes you will still get a different result.
- I know more about my site than anyone else.
- Sometimes when you have tested it long enough, you'll know more about the technology than the vendors do.

But when I started to consider how to go about getting a pay raise, it all went a bit pear-shaped. The manager's job came up for grabs, and although I did not want the job, I wanted the money. Working in a technical role seemed to have a financial cap, so I applied for the management job, fully aware at the time, that in most companies the only manager's jobs held by women were in HR.

I didn't get the job or the money, and in that moment I made a decision to become a contractor and 'chase the big bucks'. It didn't seem to matter that I was a woman, since my CV was a masterpiece of technology and the number of females working in technical positions was on the rise. With a shortage of technical expertise in the field, I always popped up on recruiter databases, and so my contracting career took off.

CHAPTER 11

Consider the Impact Upfront:
Feeling the effects of change

Most techos don't consider the impact upstream and downstream of a change they make: they simply see an issue and aspire to fix it, without considering the bigger-picture implications. Even the smallest change can cause an outage, and the data supports the statement that 90% of major outages are caused by change.

One of the key drivers of building a platform was to create a method for techos to discover what is upstream and downstream from them, to ensure that when they create a change they can identify the potential business impact. Although it may feel counterintuitive, it's crucial to communicate to the business users all the problems that a 'fix' may cause. I have observed many techos underestimate what a change will do and overestimate the control they have on how the technology layers will respond to the change. If you don't know how things are connected, then you cannot possibly know what will change when you make an alteration or what impact it will have on the customer.

On one job, my first contract nearly put me to sleep. (I hope my old client isn't reading these words, but in fact, I actually fell asleep at my desk one day due to boredom!) It was probably what most people at that organisation were used to, but after having spent seven years trailblazing with technology, focusing on changes in the Data Centre required the energy levels of only about 50% of my normal day.

In fact, my role involved keeping watch on the WAN/LAN engineers who 'played around' with the network during office hours. They reported to a different technology tower, and they didn't see the benefits of advising the upstream teams about what they were changing, and they also didn't feel any sense of responsibility for the downstream customer either. What these engineers were doing upset the mainframe and midrange teams, who by this time were very frustrated by the engineers causing all these outages. I referred to this scenario as the *cavalry versus the cowboys*.

At the time, there was no remote control on servers, so the engineers had to go to the Data Centre to make changes in person. I used to politely ask the engineers what they were going to do, which was always met with stony silence. When they wouldn't answer me, I just let them in the door and followed them around. Imagine a woman leaning over the shoulder of the silent server engineer, documenting the change and then presenting it to the manager. So began my introduction to 'cowboy change' management, in which I became an expensive but thorough secretary. As I was being well paid, I made the best of this situation for a short while. However, after three months, I needed a bigger challenge and so I moved on to the next adventure.

CHAPTER 12

Tackle One Thing at a Time:
Document problems to track issues

Documentation or a simple manual are one of the most under-utilised assets available to IT people. I have always been passionate about gaining knowledge through reading documentation and manuals. I certainly didn't want to repeat the same mistake or process twice, and I imaged that customers felt the same way. Empowering the Helpdesk with knowledge and giving them confidence to solve issues over the phone is the gold medal we always want to win.

Building a platform that captures and relays the critical technology attributes required to run an Operation was the leanest approach to Knowledge Management I could find. Recognising that IT people often have an aversion to writing and sharing, I knew it was critical to ensure the capture and maintenance of knowledge was as simple and efficient as possible. We started thinking 'outside the square' from the traditional knowledge management approach. Once a Helpdesk team has a classification system (Taxonomy) and the necessary knowledge, they gain confidence in talking to customers and fixing issues over the phone.

When I joined a Technical Support team, I was astounded at how they kept fixing the same problems over and over. They didn't have any documentation, so as the 'newbie,' I decided to document everything and hand it to the Helpdesk Operator. Ideally, the Helpdesk would then have the knowledge and resources they needed to fix these problems when they received a call, which meant that we technical people could move on to more interesting and skill-specific tasks. But when I started to notice that problems we had a fix for were still recurring, I was stumped.

I eventually worked out that when my coworkers were attempting to fix a problem, they would go through a standard set of configuration changes they believed fixed all problems. But this supposed 'fix-all' configuration would undo any subsequent fixes of issues that had arisen since the initial installation. I saw this as a band-aid to finding the source of the problem – and it was a band-aid that was making the wound worse.

My next decision was a bit radical: I asked all the technical people to do 'other things' for a few months, and the Helpdesk Operator and I handled all the calls and fixed everything. As the two of us worked together, I would document fixes as I found them and the Helpdesk Operator would test them. We eventually got to the point where the Helpdesk was able to resolve most of the issues over the phone.

One day I found a technical team member asleep in the cabling closet after a long lunch at the pub. You'd think I'd be mad; however, the customer was happy, the Helpdesk was happy, and Technical Support was definitely happy. Ultimately, a Standard Operating Environment (SOE) that was locked to a standard configuration came in, and so ended the ability to individually configure a PC and apply band-aids.

Unfortunately, not all IT people are focused on reducing problems for customers. In those days it seemed customers with IT issues were good for business, and visiting them was considered to be a social event for IT. But I was always interested in removing all the niggly IT issues that interrupted the customer, and, through research and testing, in developing new ways of doing things.

We had an IBM Mainframe at the time, and the IBM sessions always timed out. Regardless of the number of calls that came in, nobody ever really got to the bottom of it. I asked around and got answers like:

- It has always been a problem.
- Nobody seems to know what causes it.

Occasionally, I'd hear a more technical answer like:

- The load balances are configured the same but only one does it.
- Nothing changed at the desktop – they are all standard!

I decided to go back to the basics and read the manual (RTFM!). It turned out that all things pointed to a switch setting. It took me a couple of weeks to uncover the problem as this was a production environment. I then made changes and tested during maintenance windows and finally got everything to work. This issue had been plaguing this company for years, and though I never did the numbers on the cost, I can only imagine how much productive working time they had previously lost.

CHAPTER 13

The Redbook and the Hot Seat:
Test standard processes in real time

Creating an opportunity for the Technical gurus to get familiar with the Service Centre operation, answering the phone and providing valuable knowledge was my responsibility as the manager of the Service Centre. During this process, the mutual respect and relationships established between the Service Centre people and the technical gurus grew into an awesome synergy, as evidenced in achieving 90% fix on first contact, which resulted in reduced escalations and made for an enormously cohesive team.

When you have total executive support, it is possible to achieve significant skills uplift from a Helpdesk to a Service Desk to a Service Centre. Some would say this was the evolution of the team known as the IT single point of contact for the customer. I believe that along with this name change came an expectation that help would expand to an all-encompassing service to the customer, including increased accountability and an improvement in the customer experience

I created the concept of the 'Redbook,' or, a folder that contained crucial knowledge, as a tangible physical object.

Using this approach, each person in the Service Centre would receive a folder to keep all the critical information about the business and IT operation. They were expected to maintain it and ensure that they all, as a team, had the same content. I would randomly quality check the folder to make sure. My rationale behind this initiative was how can a Service Centre provide consistent customer service if each person in the Service Centre cannot manage to keep a folder in the same way.

We used the Redbook as an induction manual, and so it became the single source of 'truth' for the Service Centre and we always kept it up to date. I found a way to continually test the Redbook and keep the induction process current by means of the 'Hot Seat' process.

The 'Hot Seat' came about because we could not achieve high levels of fixes on first contact with the customer. The Service Centre told me they didn't have the access they needed to actually fix things, and they also couldn't get technical staff to explain how they fixed issues, so they did not have the information required to instruct the customers.

I got agreement from the Executive for each person in the IT department to spend a half day rostered into the Service Centre being cycled through, either monthly or quarterly, depending on what was happening overall with projects. This was not a popular decision and there was a lot of resistance. Suffice to say no one was willing to volunteer! So in order to get the ball rolling, the most senior executive volunteered. They test drove the Redbook with a 30-minute induction session, and then I let them loose on the phone. We ignored all the excuses from the rest of the IT team and scheduled them in.

While in the Hot Seat, each person was expected to document the top 10–20 issues that they'd dealt with, along with the associated fixes. The biggest benefit from this exercise was the relationships that formed between the Service Centre and the Technical gurus. Communication improved immediately, as well as an ongoing willingness to share knowledge.

CHAPTER 14

Shared Responsibility:
Shorten program timeframes and establish baselines

I have personally seen time and time again how challeng-ing it can be to run effective programs over many years in order to achieve the Return on Investment (ROI) that underpins the entire business case that initially financed the program. To address this concern, I started creating benefits that could be realised over shorter timeframes and became creative about turning business benefits into financial out-comes (either savings or revenue).

When programs run over several years, it can be dif-ficult to stay the course. It is crucial to know the baseline, or the current state, so you know your starting position. You can then track performance relative to this baseline and keep everyone involved accountable. Showing the traceability of benefits, their realisation, and all the risks involved extending beyond technology into the business operation ensures that responsibility is shared and doesn't all land in the lap of the Program Manager.

My first task as the IT Program Manager on a new contract was to shut down a large program that had been running over several years, costing several millions of dollars as part of a start-up. This meant I needed to do a program closure report.

The program closure report included identifying the original business benefits and how they traced through to realisation. As I delved into the time savings that the technology interfaces had been estimated and expected to deliver, I discovered that the data we needed to transfer through the technology interface had become subject to privacy laws. It was no longer legal to transfer the data, and therefore, the data could not be utilised as planned. I realised that the business benefit and the basis for the entire program was nonexistent. I wrestled with this for a number of weeks. The purist in me wanted to call it out, but I wasn't sure if this was really my role.

As the last person on the program and as someone who was responsible for leading the planning for a new business case, there didn't seem much point in calling out what everyone else seemed to have already accepted. Consequently, I improvised and managed to get the program shut down without drawing attention to the fact.

CHAPTER 15

Test Early and Often:
Involve the whole team

When planning new programs or projects, invariably someone will want to talk about how to reduce the budget or shorten the timeline. Many times during this discussion, there will be a question about testing, such as: Why do we need three iterations? I make sure I explain to everyone involved why it is easier to shorten the timeline when the testing goes well rather than having to experience the negative impact and disappointment of extending the timeline if the testing goes badly. My goal is to make sure it ends up incorporating three cycles of testing.

Over the years, I have discovered there is an art to testing. It requires the identification of vital business functions and the three-step method of plan, execute, repeat.

Being involved in part of a large program of work meant there was a large team of 25 people, including IT and the overall business. This also meant that there was a lot of emphasis on following a methodology whereby each person had a specific role. This was a new experience for me as previously I had been wearing all the hats. I learnt about each of the roles from some of the best operators that I had ever met. I was lucky to have joined a team of people who were willing to share their knowledge and this led to a change in my attitude. It was the first time I had worked with a real team, and this raised the bar for me. I modeled every future program of work and project with this approach: being open and honest, as well as acting with integrity and as one team.

As the 21st century loomed and everyone was nervous that Y2K would send all areas of technology into a spiral of shutdowns, we approached this uncertainty as an opportunity to validate all the work that had been achieved so far on the program. I learnt the art of enterprise testing from a Test Manager who I remain friends with to this day. I have never met anyone since who was as passionate about testing, which opened my eyes to just how important it is to sort out all the issues in testing *with the customer involved*. I discovered it was possible to have a new system go into production at 'go live' without any surprises.

That Test Manager was the first person who made it clear to me that there are no shortcuts when it comes to testing. If it is not tested, then you cannot be sure that it will work. When changes are made during testing, you must go back and test all levels of functionality to ensure one change has not broken something else.

Thorough testing is like insurance: if you don't have it, you are sure to break something. When carrying out our Y2K planning, it was essential to simulate production and build a 'like for like' environment so that the dates could be rolled forward. One issue that the Y2K testing uncovered was significant; let's just say it was a 'showstopper' that would have brought down a multi-location virtual contact centre of a major telecommunications company. Code was written well in advance to fix the issue, and a smooth rolling over of the clock occurred. It cemented for me the fact that three cycles of testing are absolutely essential.

What probably also cemented my love affair with delivering projects on time was that I was paid a $20,000 bonus during my time as an IT Program Manager. This was most unexpected, but there's nothing like a positive association between time and money to reinforce this fact!

CHAPTER 16

Business Process Mapping Builds Confidence:
The relationship between inputs and outputs

Providing a methodology and standard visual template gives the whole team confidence that their contribution will make a difference. They can see the map, and they can see how their contribution fits in to the bigger picture. Getting everyone involved and gathering their viewpoint of the world gives me confidence that nothing will be missed.

Taking a data approach makes it much easier and quicker to collate and consolidate the information, and to summarise the overall objectives of the Business Unit. The managers and executives benefit by being given an overview which they can use to drill down to inspect areas that have been tagged as potential candidates for improvement.

I was assigned the challenge of mapping all the processes for a Business Unit within a large organisation. I had completed the project I'd been engaged to deliver and had a month to spare. So in order to undertake this process efficiently, I started with all the functions within the Business Unit and mapped these to each team to confirm ownership.

When walking through the functions with the Managers and their Executives, I confirmed the Business Unit vision and mission statements, along with an agreement to provide a short description of what the Business Unit did.

Based on my belief that Managers don't always know what their team does, I also got agreement to engage every person across the Business Unit. I needed to make sure that I had all the relevant data, and I then laid out my method for approval. I explained that each person would spend 30 minutes with me as I went through the vision, mission, and short description to ensure we had an agreed starting position. I would give them a template to complete, explain how to fill it in, and be available for any questions. I would then collect the completed template in one week for review.

During the second week, I would review with each person in order to ensure I understood what they had completed. Then I'd collate and produce a draft of the business operation document by the end of the third week. In the fourth week, I would distribute and review the template with the Managers and Executives, and complete the final updates.

The key to success was creating a template that was simple, visually appealing, and that would enable me to roll up the data for a consolidated view of the Business Unit. I used the input, process, output approach and added in the relationship component. In my 30-minute sessions with each person, I asked them to consider all the inputs that they received – email, reports, requests, and systems – and then to identify the source department of the upstream relationships they had.

I then asked them to consider all the processes they performed with each of the inputs, and to consider what the outputs were. In relation to the outputs, I asked them to identify the downstream relationships – that is, those people who received the outputs.

For most people, this was the first time they considered what they did in terms of an input, process, and output with relationships. When all the data was rolled up into a Business Unit perspective, the existing overlap and inefficiencies became quite obvious, and Management could now make better educated decisions about how to respond effectively.

The 4PT Framework: PARTNERS

CHAPTER 17

Choosing Wisely:
Finding the right partner for the right service

My first experience with the word *partner* was rooted in the partnership I formed with customers early in my career. Within my first five years working in the IT industry during the late 1980s, I implemented more than 200 accounting and finance systems into small-to-medium-sized businesses. Ranging from infrastructure through to training, all the people I worked with and formed partnerships with were potential customers for ongoing IT support and maintenance.

Early on, I realised that choosing a partner was a two-way street. The prospective partners had to be a good fit for our business, have a common goal or outcome, and be able to communicate what the problem was, as well as being prepared to work with me to fix it. Ultimately, as a result of my skills in Unix and integration, I converted customers to online support and trained my staff to connect to the customers remotely (via a modem) in order to resolve IT issues ourselves.

I also formed partnerships with our suppliers, and quickly discovered that there was a large range of suppliers out in the marketplace. Unfortunately, I found very few of them had mastered the art of having a positive impact on our customers and, in those cases where other partners were involved, I often had to assume the role of customer relationship manager myself.

Choosing the right partner for a specific service, product, or infrastructure all starts with the questions of cultural fit, shared values, and how they are able to deal with such constraints as:

- budget
- executive sponsorship
- functional governance at all levels of the organisation
- availability of the necessary skilled resources
- responsiveness.

Partners who don't demonstrate a solid understanding of the value of the customer relationship in every transaction with a customer could find themselves being replaced. There used to be a time when a partner could continue to be rewarded for poor performance. However, that outdated mindset is changing within the technology culture which now tends to take a more customer-demand driven perspective. These days, a frustrated or dissatisfied customer can transition easily to a new partner from whom they can expect better and more reliable service. If a partner can retain their customers as references or case studies, the ability to continue to build on the relationship and stay aligned with any changes happening with the customer can be turned into a real competitive advantage.

When I found I was having trouble selecting a partner for a given service, I shifted my focus to finding a person inside the partner organisation with whom I thought I could work well; someone who would communicate and perform not only as a service provider, but as a true partner. It really does come down to building a team that extends outside your organisation and includes people who work together harmoniously – regardless of the organisational or employment status boundaries. You cannot assume this will simply happen by itself. I have relied on team activities and even sports to blend teams, both large and small – even in the case of teams of more than 400 people! I have gone to great lengths to find commonalities across partner organisations that might help individuals build relationships that will strengthen the team and which, in turn, will ultimately benefit the customer.

I have spent my career working between the customer's world and their service partners in the vendor and supplier world. Because I have seen both sides, I have been able to develop an understanding of just how crucial an alignment of goals can be. The customer experience will always suffer unless all partners can align their goals harmoniously.

CHAPTER 18

Selecting Your A-Grade Team:
The value of top-notch vendors

At some point during my career journey, while working for a particular partner, I made a game-changing observation: in order to win customer business, a prospective vendor or supplier will always send in their A-Grade Team. Once their top-performing employees have impressed their prospective customers and secured the business, they then begin to replace the A team members with the B, C, D, E, and F team members. I was surprised that customers were not yet aware of this fact, even though it was the 1990s by then, and many customers were riding the wave of outsourcing to partners, thinking that it would achieve better outcomes.

Establishing an outsourcing contract takes a huge amount of time, with many hours invested in forming contract relationships. So seeing these relationships dissolve as soon as the papers were signed was hugely disappointing. When I was working on the customer side, I made it my objective to keep the A Team working for us for the duration of the contract. I reasoned that their resources were a key component of the contract: quite often five-year deals would be struck, based largely on the customer's understanding of the potential partner's skills and capabilities – all represented by the skills and experience of their A Team.

I invented new ways to ensure the vendor or supplier couldn't make adjustments to the original contract. Firstly, I made sure to embed within the contract wording, the names of the people and their roles at the time of negotiation in order to guarantee we could keep them on board for the duration of the project. Secondly, I wrote clauses in the contract that prohibited a partner from changing roles without our (i.e. the customer's) consent, to be obtained only through a formal agreement process.

Any time I've held a role that involved working with outsourced partners, I have shared my knowledge about how they operate and how best to work with them in order to get the best outcomes for the customer. These partnerships are driven predominantly by sales numbers and the commercial viability of each customer account. If the customer understands and respects this, then it is their responsibility to obtain the maximum benefit from any commercial arrangement.

This takes work at any level of the customer organisation that has touch-points, or reasons for contact, with a partner. If the customer takes their 'finger off the pulse', then the partner may also see an opportunity to take their 'foot off the accelerator'.

CHAPTER 19

Changing Resources:
The importance of formal involvement

Of course, in some cases the A-Grade Team does have to move on; to different projects or to a different organisation. As a negotiator and customer advocate within the partnership, I can respect that people may be transferred, projects are reassigned, and resources change. What I am unwilling to accept, however, is not being informed of the reason behind why a partner might want to make changes. By demanding greater transparency about the reasons for these changes, I was able to stay abreast of what was going on inside the partner organisation.

For example, a partner might raise concerns about pricing, arguing that they needed to be able to be flexible and leverage resources across their organisation. However, since this was a problem that existed within their own organisation, it was not one that I was willing to let influence our end of the partnership. To formally monitor changes in contracts and to ensure I still had access to the A Team anytime a partner proposed changes, I demanded to be included in the interview panel, reviewing CVs that had been put forward, to select any replacements. I had found that partners were often very informal about how they made these reassignments and, hence, being dependent on their internal processes was not acceptable for me.

I've always explained that it was critical for me to select the right fit for the team and that the partner resources were no different. There is no room for dropping the ball when you're running an operation. One 'bad apple' and the whole team could be affected. I believe that within any organisation, people are its greatest asset, and this is even more the case in the IT industry due to its complexity. For this reason, ensuring the right people stay on the job is doubly important.

I recommend that whenever you're forming a partnership, keep an eye out for over-baked contracts. Beware of over-management which can be both costly and inefficient due to hidden fees. I was always wary of management fees, in particular, and I specifically had an issue with project management costs that were rolled into a contract or statement of work because it's often quite difficult to see what value these fees add.

Some partners will include risk or contingency or that 'little bit on top', which is meant to cover themselves just in case they made a mistake in understanding the customer requirements, and they may call that a management fee. However, it was only after I had to closely analyse such a management fee as part of a long-term contract review that I was confronted by the fact that nobody really knew what this fee was specifically for. It equated to millions of dollars wasted by a customer who was being over-managed by a vendor.

I have found it is best to regularly inspect all pricing related to the management of the contract or service delivered. The world of technology changes so rapidly that what is established one year may be completely different the next. Certainly, customer requirements change, and they also undergo changes in resources, skills, and capability, and contracted partners must be willing to align to these changing needs, or be replaced.

I closely consider the skill level of the management team and specifically identify Program or Project Management resources in order to ensure a clear understanding of their roles and responsibilities from the outset. Looking closely at who's actually doing what can expose areas where vendors are loading up costs and using people on the bench (i.e. out of the resource pool) who may not necessarily be those people with the right skill level. As a customer, I was never interested in taking on partner resources that were not the right fit, particularly if they carried their own unnecessary fees as part of the deal.

I have always treated the customer's money as though it was coming out of my own bank account. Partners sometimes found this attitude to be surprising, even confrontational; however, I never let up on squeezing out the most value or 'bang for the buck'. If I was challenged – and I often was – I would put the same question back on them by asking them if the cost was coming out of their bank account, how they would feel about paying for resources that were not up to the job? After all, one of the main reasons a customer outsources or selectively sources is to get the capability uplift from a partner they expect will do the job better than they could do it themselves.

In addition to keeping an eye on over-baked contracts, less-than-suitable resource changes, and hidden or unnecessary fees, always guard against too much red tape, which can often indicate a lack of agility. Nothing is more painful than watching a partner who is not able to meet deadlines regularly because of the red tape inside their organisation. Customers may not notice if they themselves have cumbersome and inflexible processes to deal with; however, when a customer can be agile, the partner's weaknesses in this area will show if they can't keep up.

If you experience problems in the sales process of a partner organisation as a result of lack of responsiveness to deliverables and dates, then consider that you may be getting an early insight into what the delivery process might be like. This is a huge red flag that should be further investigated.

A key criteria when selecting a partner is the alignment of how quickly the organisation adapts to change. Taking it one step further, organisations must be aligned in driving change actively in response to market demand. I often see agile organisations or organisations that need to be agile in order to survive select a partner that is 'a slow old beast'. This, for the most part, does not end well.

Lack of agility plays out in many ways, including:

- Governance meetings where the same issues are raised from meeting to meeting. The partner appears to be 'a deer in headlights' and unable to get changes made inside their organisation.

- Alterations to the contract are frowned upon, even when the current contract does not deliver the intended outcome. A partner who resists contract review and change may have an organisational structure in place that does not support being agile to customer needs.

- Operational change-management takes weeks or even months of approvals, with no commitment to dates.

- Limited resource availability holds up delivery at either the operations or projects level and has a negative impact on the customer's timeline.

- Proposals for new business are not delivered within the agreed timeframe, and customers are forced to delay decision-making, which may potentially have a negative impact on their business.
- Communication between the different levels of the organisation varies greatly.
- Technology versions are not kept up-to-date or the type of technology is not leading-edge.

In summary, selecting a partner and establishing a strong working relationship requires that a customer is willing to take on the lead role. A customer who expects their partner to be 'set-and-forget' has either found a partner who respects the relationship and will deliver beyond expectations, or they are very naïve and destined for disappointment.

Like any partnership, a vendor partnership takes effort and there will be times when it simply isn't working. In cases where the relationship has become dysfunctional and the goals are no longer commonly shared, it is best to rip off the band-aid quickly, by terminating the contract and finding a new and better aligned partner as soon as possible.

Of course, changing partners always brings with it increased costs and potential disruption to the overall operation. Whenever I have been involved in such a review, I have found that partners may be able to invigorate themselves; however, in the majority of cases it is preferable to disengage.

Putting the transition costs aside, I have seen huge leaps in performance when a customer engages a new partner. They can bring new ideas and knowledge to the table, and they are often more customer focused and more closely aligned. Before you know it, this new partner has raised the baseline by which you're measuring all your partnerships, and any other partners are now under the microscope. This can be a great opportunity for your organiation to realign its goals and re-negotiate expectations with other partners.

CHAPTER 20

Sourcing Workers:
Target skillsets and tap into experience

While every organisation has its own reasons for outsourcing, I have never had a positive view of what all too often seems to me to be an abdication of management responsibility. I understand that there can be other drivers behind the decision, but who really believes that a major outsourcer who has never run your operation would do a better job than you?

Throughout my career, I have been involved in outsourcing, insourcing, selectively sourcing, and delivering an outsourced capability, and so I have seen this process from all angles. I've come to believe there is a customer or scope size that is best suited to some forms of outsourcing, and there certainly are boutique outsourcers who do it better if they are able to bring a specialist capability to the table that ends up strengthening the overall operation. I still think it comes down to the people who head up the operation – whether this includes insourced, outsourced, or selectively sourced – and that's why regardless of your approach, you are seeking a team who are accountable and capable.

When a customer's IT department is transitioning from running the operation in a hands-on capacity to simply managing and maintaining the operation, it requires a shift in skills. Part of the preparation for outsourcing, insourcing, or selectively sourcing is to evaluate the organisational structure and re-organise where necessary. It can be particularly difficult to find those people in your team who have the management and maintenance skillset required to manage a vendor or multiple vendors successfully. I have often found that engaging a vendor can expose your capability weaknesses. The vendor will either take advantage of them or work with you to supplement them. It comes down to the alignment of values between the organisation's culture and management team.

Back in the 1990s, I worked for a CIO who re-organised his delivery organisation as part of an outsourcing decision. He identified and sourced key roles to ensure the outsourcing process would be effective and operate successfully. This required a major re-structure of the Management team, and so the CIO hired a leading recruitment company who happened to have a 'gun' headhunter on board. During this process, I was exposed to a different approach for defining and seeking specific people with the specific skillsets required.

Targeting the skillsets and finding people with deep experience in the capabilities we needed brought an injection of confidence which, in turn, created an immediate change within the organisation's culture. The new Management team was so vastly different that I never forgot the feeling of 'watching magic happen': the process of putting together a team of capable, confident, and focused leaders. This scenario changed my perspective on what is possible with partnership alliances and my approach to creating successful technology outcomes.

CHAPTER 21

The Art of Vendor Management:
Using the data to pick a side

Vendor management is the art of being the go-between for the customer and the vendor, who both often seem to be talking two completely different languages. While it's important to watch out for vendors with too many excuses, some customers will always be unhappy. Sometimes the customer is the problem and you will only be able to help them when they are desperate. The rest of the time, these types of customers are looking for someone to blame for problems that are inherent in their business. After working with customers who brought this bad attitude to the table, I really came to understand the saying that 'the fish stinks from the head down'! Solving technology issues is easy to me, but educating executives who are not technical but are unhappy about your fixes can be very challenging.

I had decided to expand my business, and after spending two months writing a business plan and completing the subsequent market research, I discovered that the market was about to crash by an estimated 30% after Y2K. So I reduced my expectations and decided not to launch headlong into an expansion but, instead, to take some time off and watch what happened over the next 12 months.

After only a three-week break, via a word of mouth request, I found myself presenting my proposal to a board of directors demonstrating how I could fix their IT department, including the current crisis they were having with their financial system and the vendor who had provided it. In this case, the customer had reached the point of referring to the contract, investigating the money they had spent, and calling in their lawyers for assistance. Their relationship with the vendor was in serious jeopardy.

The customer had not been able to send any invoices for about a month, and with several millions of dollars involved, naturally it was a heated situation. There was no silver bullet, and it took several months to sort out all of the issues. In the end, the fix required patience and focus, including daily updates and the directive that everyone remain focused on the end result and not become emotional.

As with all areas of technology, if the fix was easy, then there would have never be a problem in the first place. My investigation uncovered a number of issues that required a lot of education to properly address. The funny thing was – although it wasn't at all funny at the time – was that about six months later, I found myself as the vendor that had been out of favour with that customer. The situation had become very heated and political, but I became aware, through their apparent serial problems with their vendors, that some customers are nearly impossible to please. I did manage to sort out the problems, then closed this chapter and moved on to more genial clients.

The 4PT Framework: PROJECTS

CHAPTER 22

The Team Trained Me:
Learning program management skills

Running a program of work is a whole different ball game from many other types of consulting work. I was lucky enough to join a program team that had been running for about five years, and my predecessor was an exceptional leader. You could say that the team trained me to become a skilled Program Manager.

Some of the key lessons I learned about program management as a result of working with this team are outlined below:

- Gain Executive sponsorship (both business and IT) as early as possible as it is an essential ingredient for the program's overall success.
- Appreciate the different styles of people involved in a larger program of work.
- Keep an open mind and recognise that there are many different ways to get the job done – you might just learn something new!
- Leverage existing relationships established by different team members to save time and benefit the program.

- Work through organisational issues together by relying on the previous experience of the team members who may have solved these issues in the past.
- Use the Project team to influence the Operations team as some Project team members may have already worked in an Operations role and, hence, understand its culture.
- Establish the interdependencies and critical paths early on.

A program of work is by nature longer in duration, multi-streamed, and more complex than a simpler project, and it requires matrix management. Therefore, it's nearly impossible for the Program Manager to stay on top of each detail and every person working on the program. This requires a change in management style, whereby the Program Manager shifts more towards adopting a leadership role rather than active personnel or project management.

A key skill involved in running a successful program is the ability to paint a picture of the end game. What will it look like and what will it feel like when the program achieves its outcomes? When each person on the program understands their role in getting to the end result, then the Program Manager no longer has to manage all the details. Putting the right escalation and communication procedures into place will also ensure that the program is managed by exception in order to reduce the communication overhead.

I have seen Program Managers without the necessary subject matter expertise who are still able to deliver the right outcomes and achieve success. I believe this is because smart Program Managers put the right people with the right skills into place to manage the streams or projects within the program. In this way, having an expert team can make up for a Program Manager's lack of specific subject knowledge. Nevertheless, a Program Manager who does have the subject matter expertise can enjoy imparting that knowledge to their team, as well as growing their own skillset.

When you have experience in running programs, it is easier to get a head-start on issues, to mitigate risk, and to avoid many of the traps that can occur throughout the life of a program. I have also found it very valuable to share my list of issues and risks with the team early on and get their input on the best mitigation tactics. Soliciting the team's input at the beginning can also shed light on the organisation's history and culture, both of which may also have an impact on the overall success of the program.

Leading a program can be very fulfilling, but is not for the faint-hearted. It requires you to focus on your leadership style and may require some adjustments from your typical approach to being a Project Manager. I have found that people skills play a key role in your success as an influencer. I recommend that anyone considering moving into a program management role read up on human behavior, in particular via such books as *How to Win Friends and Influence People* by Dale Carnegie.

Projects are founded on a methodology, and throughout my time working in the IT industry, I have been exposed to many methodologies – some adopted and some homegrown. Methods all have their own positives and negatives, so the key to selecting a methodology or building one from the outset is getting the right cultural fit and speed aligned to the organisation.

CHAPTER 23

The Knight in Shining Armour:
Following a PRINCE2 training style

B ack in the late 1990s, many organisations were considering outsourcing as a way of appearing more attractive
for acquisition. I helped prepare one organisation to make
that move. As part of the partnership arrangement with the
outsourcer, they introduced the PRINCE2 methodology and
training all the staff and contractors was part of this deal.

PRINCE2 (Projects In Controlled Environments) is a
structured project management method, originally developed
by the UK government, which emphasises dividing projects
into manageable and controllable stages.

By adopting the PRINCE2 method, I discovered that
project management could be kept really simple. I learnt
about the importance of clear roles in the control board,
managing by exception, and setting clear boundaries and
constraints that the Project Manager could work within.

The most enlightening part of this method, though,
was the importance of having clarity around the roles within
the control board or stakeholder group. This has continued
to influence my approach whenever I encounter experienced

stakeholders who want to assume multiple roles on a project. They're often driven innocently enough by their interest or experience in a particular technology or business area. However, having the same person involved in multiple roles can be very dangerous for the Project Manager and can lead to delays in decision-making and, ultimately, the project timeline.

The concept of managing by exception had an impact on my project management style. I realised it was my responsibility to come to an agreement with the control board at the outset regarding the boundaries and constraints of the project. This initiative enabled me to focus on the delivery of the project rather than deciding what needed to be escalated, to whom, and how.

I did find that the PRINCE2 methodology included lots of templates; however, completing these taught me I had to be more succinct which, in turn, improved my written communication skills. I also realised that being able to take complex, highly technical details and roll these up into an easily consumable and readable project brief was something of an artform, and not one that not many technology people can do well.

From then on, whenever I have arrived in a new organisation that does not have a methodology already in place I always recommend they consider using PRINCE2. I'm then able to get started straightaway by applying a simplified version. This always provides an easy-to-follow structure and templates, and offers an immediate boost in confidence around the project's overall success.

CHAPTER 24

Project Management Body of Knowledge:
Bring on the methodology

There are many ways of saying the same thing, but there's a definite advantage in having clarity of communication with everyone in an organisation speaking the same language. That's the benefit that Project Management Body of Knowledge (PMBOK) brings to project management. Offering a set of standard terminology and guidelines (republished every few years in an updated volume) that aim to keep up with rapidly-changing technology, PMBOK lays out a vocabulary and framework for thinking about project management.

My initial introduction to PMBOK quickly increased my awareness of all the components of a project, as well as the theory behind it. I'm a detail-orientated person who was being paid to follow the method, so I jumped in boots (or high heels!) and all. I carefully went through all the phases and templates, and I was able to tick all the boxes. I certainly made sure the Project Management Office was happy with my project management skills.

While I enjoyed acquiring all this new knowledge, I was aware that following the PMBOK methodology would not necessarily lead to the delivery of a successful project. I watched Project Managers follow the method and still struggle to meet the usual criteria for success: positive business outcomes and return on investment. With forty-seven processes embedded into the PMBOK methodology, grouped into five process groups and ten knowledge areas, the sheer volume of knowledge can be overwhelming. However, I did work out how to make the project artifacts match my project success in order to keep everyone happy.

One of the key outcomes of learning this methodology was the concept of input, process (referred to as tools and techniques), and output. I quickly latched onto this concept and later used it as an approach to fast-track documenting the Operating Manual for a business unit or department. This helped me quickly work out what level of organisational change my project was going to create, what would be key to the project's success, and how we would sustain change after the project was completed.

CHAPTER 25

Sprints and Scrums:
The power of 90-day agility cycles

When I first came across the Agile Methodology following many years operating in the role of a Project and Program Manager, I was surprised to discover that I had already implemented many of its characteristics into my personal working style. I realised that I was able to be really focused and motivated for about three months, and then I required a break. I would book a week off every three months in order to escape to a place on the planet I had not previously travelled to. I found that when I returned from my holiday, I felt invigorated and ready to tackle the next three months.

I started to refer to three months as 90 days (not working days, just the number of calendar days), and when I started looking more closely, I discovered that every 90 days was a line in the sand for my team as well. A team of people can achieve amazing outcomes in 90 days, so I began to break up the project deliverables to fit within the 90-day boundary and ensure that everyone on or involved with the project was working to this timeline. I always emphasised the fact that the date was immovable as I was going away on a holiday!

It offered the team an endpoint to work towards as well. Even if they weren't all leaving the country, it provided team members with a deadline date to aspire to and check off.

I also thought that I'd invented the daily stand-up meeting: the concept of a quick daily meeting where the whole project team (including Operations people) came together to increase engagement and alignment. I was so passionate about this activity that when it became an official recommendation in the Agile methodology, I was delighted. I had seen the numerous benefits whenever I ran transformation programs with multiple streams, where people were working in operational roles. It was easy for them to get distracted and absorbed into the old way of doing things, so a daily meeting was a quick, simple way to keep reinforcing a new approach.

Over the years, I came to view the daily standup meeting as an opportunity for me to communicate what was going on more broadly in the organisation, and this drove me to keep on top of new and interesting things that the team may not have already known. I reasoned that if the manager is not communicating something new with their team every day, then they can become disconnected and miss opportunities. After all, as a manager you are responsible for your team, including ensuring they are able to grow and progress in their careers and as people.

There are so many benefits to this brief, daily time with the team, including:

- Time for the Manager or Team Leader to think, before the stand-up meeting, about the most important thing they can share that day.
- Allowing team members (who often work in their own space and rarely get to mix with everyone daily) to get to know each other better. Team members form new friendships when given the opportunity to do so.

- Empowering team members to share knowledge based on skills and experience unknown to the manager or the other team members, which may come in handy during the project.
- Improved communication skills and increased confidence through active involvement in the team's activities.
- Contributions made within the team, as each person is asked to talk about what they would focus on that day.
- Opportunity to track the progress of project tasks and ensure no one person has become side-tracked which, in turn, could have an impact on the project's deliverables.
- Educating the team about how to deal with change by talking about the ways in which each person copes with and reacts to change.
- Opportunity to ask team members what skills they want to learn (either during or outside of work) and, if possible, build this into their work life.
- Opportunity to involve the whole team and harness the power of the collective knowledge and experience to deal with issues.
- Establishing an honest and open forum for resolving conflicts.
- Increased respect for differences among teammates.
- Opportunity to celebrate the smaller wins and find something to celebrate daily.
- Opportunity to determine who should receive the Star of the Week Award.

I believe that 'sprints and scrums' are a fundamental aspect of the success of any project. Keeping people focused and accountable for smaller chunks of a project and meeting daily (at the beginning of the day) supports them and provides guidance. Ultimately, by adopting this approach you will ensure that you increase the chances of meeting the goals of the project, program and organisation.

CHAPTER 26

Project Management versus Service Management:
Observing the similarities

S ome aspects of projects and their solution delivery life-cycle seemed to be so standardised that I'd always taken them for granted. Then, I found myself in an environment that was introducing selective sourcing which, in turn, led to a new – and creative – challenge for me to develop an innovative process for on-boarding partners that would ultimately span multiple partners and systems. I had to introduce the new process, pilot it, sell it, get it approved for release, train project managers how to use it, launch it, and finally, assess it in operation.

This required a lot of dedication and commitment on my part. It took two of us nine months to get approval to embed the process into the solution delivery lifecycle which, in turn, enabled all PMs to improve their capability in handing over projects based on a Service-Orientated Architecture.

For me, this scenario is where the Project Management Office (PMO) meets the Service Management Office (SMO). Even though they are coming at the process from two different perspectives and often talking two languages, their end goals are aligned in service of the business needs of an organisation. I have found that the SMO requires many of the skills and rigor that exists in a PMO, and wherever these are lacking, the success of the SMO is limited.

A few commonalities between the PMO and SMO offices (who often consider themselves to be very different!) are listed in the table on the following pages:

Description	PMO	SMO
Definition	A Project Management Office (PMO) is a group or department within a business, agency, or enterprise that defines and maintains standards for project management within the organisation. The PMO strives to standardise and introduce economies of repetition in the execution of projects. The PMO is the source of documentation, guidance and metrics on the practice of project management and execution.	The Service Management Office (SMO) is a shared service responsibility for the integration, promotion, and delivery of good (or best) practices. *OR* The Service Management Office (SMO) provides the governance structure that applies this best practice across the service management lifecycle.
Goal	To drive Project Excellence from a central group who are measured on achieving results	To drive Service Excellence from a central group who are measured on achieving improvements
Skills	Program / Project Manager Business Analyst Solution Architect Test Manager	Manager Process Manager Service Architect Reporting Manager

Planning	Project Plan	Service Management Plan, Continual Service Improvement
Focus	Project Delivery	Customer Experience
Repeatable method	Project Lifecycle	Service Lifecycle
Tracking	Project Tasks	Change and Release
Knowledge	Knowledge Articles	Known Errors
Some Common Issues	<ul><li>No clear ownership of the relationship with the business</li><li>Competition for resource allocation</li><li>Flawed service design not aligned to service management standards</li><li>Limited capability to support the new service</li><li>No list of known errors to reference when customers call.</li><li>Knowledge not transferred from Project to Operations.</li></ul>	

CHAPTER 27

Understanding a Problem to Solve it:

Baseline data produces realistic outcomes

Transformation requires agreement on the starting position. It's never more important to establish a baseline agreement than when you have 25 stakeholders who all have a different perspective, different drivers, and a different opinion on what needs to be fixed.

Even a small degree of improvement can alter the mood and tempo of a transformation. However, without knowing the starting position, it's not possible to measure progress. This is the biggest killer of momentum and motivation that I have observed. Many transformations set themselves up for failure by not establishing the baseline and then, once you start making changes, there is no going back. People forget quite quickly how things used to be once they have changed, and without any available data, there is no evidence or reference point.

The starting position has to be derived from the data to demonstrate that you have an understanding of the problem. Conducting a session with the stakeholders so that they can tell you about all the issues and what they think needs to be fixed does indicate the potential scope of the project. This also helps identify the data that needs to be gathered to ensure it supports what the stakeholders are saying. Establishing the measures for progress and agreeing on what 'great' looks like – that is, how you'll know when the transformation has been a success – is critical. Completing this step is well worth the time required for all stakeholders to discuss and agree on what measures will be applied to the data.

Agreement on the measures and asking questions about how they are calculated can unravel years of problems that have been buried or used as excuses to not move forward and remain stuck in the past. Working through these challenges until everyone reaches total agreement means that these measures and calculations can then be applied to the data after the baseline performance is clearly understood. There is absolutely no point in continuing the project until this is resolved. It can get messy. Analysing data and looking for the baseline sometimes brings past reporting on performance into question. But, as the saying from Alcoholics Anonymous (AA) states: 'Unless you admit you have a problem, you cannot solve it'.

The next step is to agree upon realistic goals for improvement. The immediate challenge when dealing with such a large group of stakeholders is that it requires all of them – and their teams – to focus on setting a new baseline to be achieved. Even when they have been stuck for years, it remains true that people don't like to change, so there is likely to be a significant amount of work to do in bringing everyone along for the ride.

Engagement must happen at all layers of the organisational hierarchy and each layer requires a different approach. Some of the ways I manage engagement at different organisational layers are outlined in the following pages:

Sponsors – Risk

The sponsors can make decisions along the way to transformation that have an impact on the new baseline. Calling this out as a risk at the start will raise awareness and reduce the possibility of sponsors influencing the agreed baseline targets. Also agreeing on how these changes will be discussed and handled means that, as a Program Manager, you can increase your ability to hit the targets.

Stakeholders – Attendance, Collaboration, Deliverables

I have always established a method of mapping and measuring attendance, collaboration, and deliverables for each stakeholder. I have experienced huge leaps in engagement whenever I publish this information to all stakeholders; starting with engagement as low as 33% to achieving over 50% in one month.

Project Team – Visible Outcomes

Agreeing on and discussing the project outcome is important, but it's not for everyone. Whether someone should be part of this conversation depends upon whether that person is a big-picture or small-picture person. Yet, once the outcome is set, it is critical that everyone gets clarity about what each project outcome means to them, as well as what they will contribute and how.

Knowing the critical success factors for the project and making these visible to everyone will be motivating for some people, while others may find it intimidating. Some team members may require more discussion to get them totally onboard, and it is worth spending that time in the early stages of the project to ensure they're prepared to make the necessary contribution before there's any chance their hesitation may have a negative impact on the project.

Management and Team Leaders – Agreed-upon, Published, Reported Deliverables

Deliverables must be agreed upon, published, and reported in order for a project team to work in harmony with operational managers and team leaders. Providing a monthly calendar of agreed deliverables for the project ensures that the project respects the workload of the operational managers and team leaders, and vice versa. This is particularly important so that each team has an understanding of what the other must achieve and by when.

Operational Teams – Performance Reporting

Reporting on performance has always inspired improved results; I view it as a way of tapping into the human desire to want to make progress towards a set target. Reporting can also uncover how the data can be manipulated and appear to meet the target. In most cases, when a person must achieve an objective publicly they will find a way to report that they've succeeded – some in the spirit it was intended and others not so much.

It is amazing how few people are clear about the scope and performance of the area in which they operate. I always start with the basics: how many people work in the department; do they have a job description; do they have performance objectives; and do they all work in the position that matches their job description or their skillset?

Starting with the basic people data is an indication of an organisation's culture and their processes around measuring. It also is an indicator of how much work lies ahead of the project in order to work through any resistance and to affect eventual change. There is a relationship between organisational culture and the project timeline, and this must be factored in to the project plan and schedule.

Many projects produce great deliverables. However, the real measure of the success of a project is the transition from project into business as usual, when you can truly realise the transformational benefits.

The 4PT Framework:
TECHNOLOGY

CHAPTER 28

The Right Tool for the Job:
Implementing technology to streamline SIAM

The technology that underpins Service Integration and Management is really no different from the technology that underpins any other department processes. Consider payroll as an example. In payroll, it is crucial to understand business requirements, document them and convert them into functional requirements based on the technology selected, and to make adjustments where necessary. It's so important because people need to get paid. But the same is true of technology across all departments, which is where a few guiding principles can ensure successful Service Integration and Management (SIAM) transitions which seamlessly integrate new technology, regardless of the department.

During my career, I have led seventeen Service Management tool implementations and introduced a variety of applications, including: Notes Customised, Helpdesk Systems, Infra, Tivoli, CA Unicentre, Heat, HP Service Centre, HP Service Manager, ServiceNow, and Remedy. These projects have all varied in size with the largest number of IT users being just under 1,500.

It may sound crazy to suggest that, regardless of their size, these projects were basically all the same. However, after completing seventeen of them, I came to realise that what makes a tool implementation successful has nothing to do with the tool itself and everything to do with prioritising what the customer needs. I always start with the customer's business requirements and help produce the reports that they'll need to measure their performance well before we start talking about which tools will work.

A key component to the potential success of a service management tool in delivering improvements is your familiarity with it. I always make sure I am able to walk-through exactly how I expect the system to meet the customer's business requirements while, at the same time, supporting their processes. I develop multiple test cases to ensure I can trace the requirements all the way until the technology delivers the outcome.

Service Management tool implementations can be a minefield. Bridging the gap between what the software vendor sells and what the customer requires can be difficult. Customers have problems and vendors have solutions; however, the challenge is to properly understand the customer's business by delivering the software to support the processes without huge customisation and ongoing maintenance costs.

It's true that many tool implementations fail. After years of making a career out of fixing them, I've identified a list of key reasons why they might not work. In addition to naming the risks and challenges, after mitigating them across seventeen successful implementations, I've pinpointed various strategies for addressing them. The main reason is the data but the rest are equally important to achieving success.

Data

Bad or poorly organised foundational data is the Number One reason for failure.

Many customers simply do not know how to organise their data properly, how the types of data are related and how to map it into a tool to get the best result.

This process of identifying, collating, analysing, validating, consolidating and normalising the data can take months of work. As part of this process, it is important to identify who will be in charge of the data moving forward. Ascertain whether the owner(s) will agree to their role and set guidelines for future governance and maintenance of the data.

Developing a service model and mapping it to the data dictionary of the tool is the most effective way to mitigate the risk of a failed implementation. Over the years, I have developed a Service Model and a Service Modelling Framework that takes away the mystery of figuring out this information.

Executive Sponsorship

Without the executive sponsorship and priority, it is almost impossible to deliver business benefits.

The project needs to be the number one (or, at a minimum, the number two) priority in the department or the business. The benefits are always focused on, and thus dependent on, operational change which, in turn, is driven by integration, automation, and being more efficient.

Often, this involves cross-functional change, so finding a strong executive sponsor is always critical to the success of the tools implementation.

Organisational Change

A realistic estimate of the impact the change will have is a key component to the success of the project; unrealistic expectations are likely to lead to results that look like failure, regardless.

Any changes – whether to personnel or processes – and particularly those changes in high volume transaction areas will require training, even if those changes appear to be small. Often, ongoing coaching is the best way to ensure the target state becomes the new current state, and that everyone is clear on what outcome will mean the project has been successful.

Functional Specification

Small details can mean the difference between the success or failure of a project.

A Functional Specification is a great mechanism to translate the Business Requirements into the details of how a system will meet those requirements, and how the constraints of the selected system will play out.

The process requires all project team members to be in the same room to flesh out the details while being aware that this may take several days. I make sure that I never skip this important step.

At the end of the process, the technical people who will be configuring or customising the system must have documented (and be able to explain in detail) how the system will work to meet the customer's requirements.

Remember – 'the devil is in the detail'.

Workflow

There is a direct relationship between the integrity of the tool and how much of the workflow is built into the tool.

Of course, this process comes at the cost of customisation.

I recommend keeping processes simple and reducing the amount of customisation involved. Removing functionality from the tool until the process matures is a more reliable approach, thereby making allowance for the tool's features to develop alongside the changing process.

Training

The quality of the training will ultimately determine the quality of data and reporting.

Embedding the process, workflow, data ownership, and reporting into the actual training program has always yielded enormous benefits. I use training as an opportunity to revisit processes as well as the relationship to data and reporting. Decisions are made from data so it's key for everyone to understand that 'garbage in' really does mean 'garbage out' – that is, that bad reporting will lead to poorly informed decisions.

As ITIL and the subsequent training programs about it grew in popularity, I watched too many people undertake ITIL training without a clear understanding of how it was being implemented into their organisation. I was distressed to see people with new knowledge about a framework incorrectly attempting to apply it in their role.

It isn't helpful for people to be able to simply pass an exam on a new theory. Instead, critical to the return on investment, it is important that they are trained less on the actual framework and more on the specifics of its adoption within their organisation.

Automation

Failure to automate where possible can result in the failure of a project.

People make mistakes so most customised automation comes with major benefits.

By automating processes you are assured that the process has been analysed and, in most cases, well documented. I struggle to understand why there is so little automation in place in modern technology.

The less human intervention in a process, the less room there is for error – particularly in the case of a process that involves numerous handoffs between departments.

Project Management

Poor project management, including unclear leadership and accountability, are other factors responsible for project failure.

The customer must lead the project, and the Project Manager must have a dotted reporting line to the PMO.

Tracing the business requirements through to delivery (including producing test cases and examples), along with the creation of a 12-month release plan ensures that expectation of delivering functionality is monitored and measured.

The project schedule must be adequately supported by IT Operations staff. Keep in mind that availability of staffing resources will ultimately have an impact on the duration of the project.

CHAPTER 29

Test and Retest:
Using data to operationalise

Everyone sees ITIL from their own perspective and based on their own experience. Connecting the dots between the people, process, partners, projects and technology is critical to the success of operationalising ITIL – and of the project as a whole. Although data can seem overwhelming at times, if each person is willing to take responsibility for their part, managing data quality becomes a much less daunting task.

I was given the opportunity to build a Contact Centre for an organisation, including additional roles for service management. This was a change from the early days of ITIL in Australia, when operational team leaders managed the people, process, and the tools. Adding service managers would be a game changer.

Working with the Human Resources team, I prepared job descriptions for the new roles. Beginning with the standard template, I added the required capabilities and behavior specific to a candidate's ability to influence teams across operations, applications and project delivery. Getting these parameters right at the outset creates a clear job scope, performance objectives, and reporting measures. With HR involved early on, we were prepared for staff to go directly to them if they had concerns, and HR were an enormous help throughout the project.

A strong relationship with HR is invaluable in managing people when organisational change is planned. It is extremely important to be familiar with the specific approach each organisation has to HR management. For a manager, HR can serve as a sounding board and provide support when introducing Service Integration and Management, as well as the necessary cultural changes and measures that come with it. I often think of the relationship between HR and management as playing 'good cop' and 'bad cop'.

Each role in the ITIL framework considers service delivery from different perspectives or through different lenses, and views the same transaction in different ways.

As an example, using the customer reporting a fault as a transaction, some ways each role can view the same transaction are described below:

A Service Level Manager asks questions about the transaction including:

- Was it within Service Level Agreement (SLA)?
- Did the SLA meet the expectation of the customer?
- Was the correct SLA applied?
- Did it get resolved at first level, how many people handled the transaction?
- What was the cost?

An Incident Manager is more interested in:

- How many customers are affected?
- Is this a high-priority issue?
- Is the customer up and running?

- Was it resolved at first level?
- Was it escalated to the right team if unresolved?

A Knowledge Manager wants to know:

- Was knowledge used to solve this issue?
- If not, was knowledge created?

A Problem Manager needs to know:

- Was there a workaround?
- Is root cause analysis required?
- What is the age of the issue?
- Has it happened before and is it recurring?
- Do the volumes or repeats suggest the problem is a trend?
- Are others experiencing the same issue?

A Change Manager investigates:

- Was the issue caused by a change?
- Is there a change planned to resolve it?

A Configuration Manager looks at how the issue relates to configuration items such as :

- Does the customer have a related asset (Configuration Item)?
- Is this a configuration item that keeps failing?
- Is it a hardware asset, and has it passed its warranty?
- Is it a software asset, and is the software licensed?

Ensuring the right person is in the right role becomes even more important with the separation of roles. Some personality attributes are certainly better suited to different roles.

Some characteristics commonly associated with these roles are listed in the following table:

Service-Level Manager	Empathetic, facilitator, outgoing, organised
Incident Manager	Accountable, optimistic, adaptable
Knowledge Manager	Thorough, creative, a reader
Problem Manager	Curious, patient, an investigator
Change Manager	Coordinator, auditor, completer
Configuration/Asset Manager	Analyst, lateral thinker, designer

Over the years, I have watched organisations put the wrong personality type into the wrong job. This creates the wrong behaviors and results in the wrong outcomes – not to mention, poor-quality data. The ITIL library appears to be missing books on People and Data; two of the most difficult parts to understand.

After consolidating five Helpdesks into a Service Centre based on ITIL, I came to the conclusion that Incident Management (issue resolution) was easier to consolidate than Service Requests (order/request fulfillment). I took the opportunity to resolve this difference between Incident as compared to Service Requests by creating a separate team to handle the Service Requests. Not only is it completely different type of work, more administration-focused, but the personalities who were attracted to this type of work were very different to those interested in Incident Management. Separating these pieces made it much easier to consolidate the workflow and look for opportunities to transform the Service Request processes to achieve significant efficiencies and improve the customer experience.

With five different Incident teams, getting each Incident team mix right with the right team leader took some time and required a number of people moves. Before making any moves, I considered the team members' results and reviewed them with the Team Leaders. The key here was to create an environment where moving was not considered a bad thing but instead an opportunity to improve. The result was increased team performance, reduced staff issues, and improved customer satisfaction.

Separating workloads and queues based on skills worked initially, and this made everyone feel comfortable with the size of the workload. But after the teams built confidence, we put the teams through cross-skilled training and moved to an all-in-one-queue, which made the work more interesting.

I focused heavily on the data that was produced and would appear on reports. I worked with the Managers and Team Leaders to create daily, weekly, and monthly objectives – and to ensure that they were measureable. I asked them to do the same with their teams, too. Complete transparency confirms that each person understands how their part in the reporting relates to their performance, which drives increased accountability and confidence.

CHAPTER 30

How Workflow Protects Data:
Understanding functional requirements

When an IT Department implements applications for themselves, it's not uncommon for the need to preserve data to be overlooked. Over the years, I have taught many people how to deliver functional requirements through a document called a Functional Specification (which covers requirements, design, and use cases).

Getting the team together with the people who will use the system and walking through each function does take time; however, it makes all the difference when everything is clarified, with no room left for assumptions or 'grey areas' which open to interpretation. I've also noticed that when the team understands the goal or the outcome they want to achieve, they come up with improvements by providing different options. The best way for them to do this is via proto-type. All Service Integration and Management tools have a multitude of options, and finding the most appropriate one is the key to matching the technology with the capability of the team.

I discovered the power of workflow when asked to build a multi-tenant service management system that would reach into the application and technical support of the customer's organisation. I wanted it to be simple and obvious, with minimal fields required, and I repeated this like a mantra.

When a tool is already in operation, there is not a lot of support for gathering business requirements, so I decided to go straight to the functional requirements. We listed all the business processes and outlined how each step of the process is executed so we were sure we were clear about the workflow. Next, we converted these lists and outlines into diagrams, and the workflow was validated.

This sounds simple enough, but it can take time, and it can certainly test the patience of everyone involved. When a person has been performing the steps in a process for a long time, they tend to forget why each step is important and often skip some. This in turn has a major impact on the data and its lifecycle.

After the diagrams, our next step was to walk through the tool, field by field, to understand how it behaved. There is a balance between adjusting the process and customising the tool, and this is where the tools team and process people must work together to better understand each other's perspective. This process is best done interactively to reduce the overall timeframe. I have tried a number of different approaches and found that allocating this time together in the beginning reduces design and test effort, and it also mitigates future disappointment.

Removing all unnecessary clutter is really important for a distributed system involving customers. You want to make each field absolutely critical so the users of the system understand how each field plays a part in the reporting process. This dramatically increases the quality of the data, as does ensuring that everyone knows who gets the report and what decisions they'll be making as a result. Knowledge really does help people to take the data seriously.

CHAPTER 31

All Types of Data are Useful:
Comprehending how and why they were created

When you start to really measure productivity, you can be more realistic about staff numbers and gain an insight into what the customer is experiencing. This not only applies to the Service Centre but to all resources delivering support services to a customer. Whenever customer satisfaction levels are low, I investigate the staff roster – but, more importantly, adherence to it.

I have experienced resource productivity as low as 50% and when I have put the data together to confirm this percentage, everyone looks surprised. I see this as being a starting position and then put actions in place in order to increase it. When people see the science behind the numbers, it is amazing how quickly productivity improves without any other changes. This point continues to prove to me that people are not really measuring or they have no faith in their measurement process.

On one occasion, I was given the challenging task of removing 20% of people from a large team as part of a program of work to cut operational costs. During this project, I learnt the value of having a staffing roster and measuring adherence to it, both for the Service Desk and Technical Support. I needed to gather the data and find out if there were areas that were actually overstaffed in order to understand what would be the result of removing 20% of the team.

I discovered that most of the IT people were not working to a support roster and created their own flexible working hours to suit themselves. This flexible approach didn't seem to be in-line with customer demand when I started looking closely at the data, which showed:

- call wait time > 30 seconds
- the abandonment rate > 5%
- customers reporting that they never got through
- once the customer logs the problem they say they never hear back from the IT team.

It seemed difficult to pin poor customer experience to a roster when you think that you have enough people, but it was definitely a red flag. The flexibility that people worked into the roster was not only for the starting and finishing times, but also about what happens in between.

Enter, Workforce Management: the true approach to understanding and measuring productivity. Starting with Erlang C, I explained how the numbers worked to the team. Erlang is the scientist who is credited with creating a method and tool to predict the resources required for each 30-minute period to answer an inbound call volume so that a call-answer target could be reached. This has been the basis of my ability to achieve increased productivity by optimising a roster to meet the daily and weekly distribution of phone calls. I look at the trends over a month, quarter, and year. Putting the roster into the Workforce Management tool and then comparing it to actual hours available for work proved to be very enlightening.

This method also forces Managers to understand and break down the workload of their team, and how they compare to the industry as a whole. Doing the analysis helps answer a number of questions, such as:

- What is the average talk time per incident and can these be separated into short (1–2 minutes e.g. passwords), medium (3–5 minutes e.g. standard known errors) and long (6–12 minutes e.g. complex new errors) or more than 12 minutes?
- What is the highest/lowest volume per person per day?
- What is the peak volume per day, per week, and per month?
- What is the percentage of available hours compared to hours scheduled?

For Managers to develop an understanding of these answers is key to understanding Service Centre productivity.

CHAPTER 32

Being Prepared for Change versus Wanting It:
Data analysis is key

B eing ready for significant change is different from wanting to change. Preparing for and achieving significant change is closely linked to the buy-in of the people. Having a science behind the change means your people will be more accepting, be involved in the change, and help to drive the outcomes. Ensuring that there is no loss in capability across multiple organisations is the ultimate plan in my opinion.

When consolidating IT departments, one of the key considerations regarding how much consolidation is realistic in the beginning is the gap in culture between different organisations. Doing the analysis on how they each deliver services prior to embarking on consolidation enables the establishment of clear outcomes and expectations.

I have witnessed a number of organisations agree on a process and then implement it in different ways. This can even occur when they're following a common framework and using the same tool. So what really makes the difference?

The difference is the necessary data and a leadership team that includes all the stakeholders who are empowered to make decisions when they're provided with the underpinning data. Without all the key ingredients, the cake comes out flat.

A key skill for a Program Manager is the ability to take detailed and complex issues that inevitably arise in a program of work, then collect all the relevant data, and distill these into options that lead to outcomes. Whenever I find myself having to think about the detail and then step back and present a summary, it works best to have a leader to bounce off and get feedback. In IT there are often so many different ways to 'skin a cat' and it's unlikely that one person knows everything. Having a 'sparring' partner has helped me to produce some of my best work!

Strong analysis skills are critical to driving real change. (If you don't have these skills yourself, make sure you hire someone who does!)

Whenever I have joined an organisation in order to deliver a project, one of the common themes is the frustration of managers and staff who are unable to influence the Executive. I invariably find that what they are presenting to the Executive is neither founded on solid analysis nor summarised to elicit interest. Once managers and staff understand that they are accountable for influencing executives, they can develop the necessary skills and improve their ability to drive decision-making and affect change. Presenting evidence in the form of data rolled up into a set of options with benefits and risks helps executives understand the challenges and make informed decisions.

CHAPTER 33

Plan Prior to Implementation:
Data walkthroughs underpin service levels

In all the projects I worked on where there were service levels involved, I included myself at the beginning, during the discussion, and at the end, to ensure that they arrived in shape to be operationalised.

It was during the renegotiation of a major outsourcing contract when I first truly understood that few people know how to meet customer expectations in outsourced environments. I worked for three months to bring the Executive up to speed on the skills required to negotiate with a vendor. Putting together a service-level agreement is the easy part. Let's face it, it's not rocket science; it's all been done before. The challenge is operationalising the service levels so that they achieve a great customer experience, which can be measured and reported on.

The first step in getting a service-level agreement to work for you is to use language that people understand. It sounds simple in theory; however, I have had to interpret a number of contracts over the years so I decided that if I was to write one then it had to be easy to read – a bit like a bedtime story with a happy ending.

Secondly, I always found it weird that the process of developing and implementing a service-level agreement excluded the people who were going to deliver it. The other strange aspect to this process was that after the details of the service levels were agreed upon, with the operational characteristics already built in, the legal team would come in and make changes. It is not an easy exercise to remove your operational people from the day-to-day pressures of operations to participate in the establishment and negotiation of service-level agreements. However, many great contracts and vendors have become untenable when they are not involved in this step.

Thirdly, having a large degree of focus on the data, how it is exchanged, who owns it, and who is accountable through its lifecycle will ensure that all the issues come to the surface and are resolved during the negotiation. Once this phase passes, it can be almost impossible to make additional changes for the life of the contract. However, I must say that this situation has changed recently and many contracts between customers and vendors are being entered into with the idea that they are somewhat flexible to meet the changing needs of the business.

The significant aspect at the end of this process is always the training. If you can walk through and simulate a service level being met, then it can be delivered. Practice makes possible.

PUTTING IT ALL TOGETHER:

Developing a framework and a digital lifecycle manangement system for Service Integration and Management (SIAM)

'The pathway to driving alignment between the IT department and the Business via a powerful Service Catalogue ... fast!'

CHAPTER 34

Mapping and Service Integration:
Creating a Service Management Plan

Developing a process within an organisation which spans all of the capabilities (towers) in the IT department, includes vendors, and reaches into the business takes months of careful planning. This is because each person sees the same process differently, as well as how it will affect them in different ways.

Embedding the process within the company is a sales and marketing exercise, which involves significant engagement, and requires all of the managers and their teams to agree on changing the way in which they currently do things. Having key outputs that the leadership team could inspect ensures that there are quality measures in place and guarantees that the process is being followed properly. Over time, the new process will become the new way of doing things.

The integration of vendors is a much easier exercise. Generally speaking, I have found that in situations where the customer takes responsibility for their 'Service Model' and clearly defines exactly what data they need from a vendor, as well as specifying how they want the data to be delivered, that vendor/s will be willing to comply. This is a specialist skill that can be scarce within the customer environment.

For the past five years, my focus has been on creating a standard 'Service Model' that customers can build on and customise to their own requirements. I believe that helping customers establish this core capability is the evolution of technology.

When you get an opportunity to work on leading-edge projects, you always hope they don't turn into 'bleeding edge' ones! On one occasion, I was asked to write a process specification for on-boarding a new vendor, which sounded like heaven to me! There was no process document template available so I had to create one. I have always jumped at the opportunity to use my writing skills in projects; whenever I'm given the time to create a template, I feel excited by the challenge.

In this case, I wrote the Service Level Management process document in such a way as to include every piece of information that could potentially be essential to know about a service. I reviewed every process across Technology and identified every attribute within the process and characteristics of that attribute. These totalled around 130, and although this felt like a work of art, it was not something that would be workable operationally. I needed to trim it down.

I came up with a core set of attributes that would enable a new service to be defined and functional under contract – eventually this document became known as the Service Management Plan. I worked closely with the Vendor Management Office in order to validate the document, and over the timeframe of several months, it was socialised with the Technology Architects. It became apparent to me that the only way to cement the Service Level Management process across the organisation was to start with all the possible entry points for new services, as well as all the ways that a service could be altered.

Given the size and complexity of the organisation, I decided to embark on a Proof of Concept (POC) and identify a critical business and technology project to test-drive the Service Level Management process. I was able to locate a willing candidate in the form of a well-respected Project Manager, who was delivering a new service that was both complex and customer-facing.

At the end of the POC, it was agreed that the Service Management Plan was a key deliverable for every project where there was a new or significantly changing service. It was embedded into the solution delivery lifecycle and became part of the standard methodology for the organisation.

With the Service Management Plan in place, the next step was to engage the vendors and create an electronic interface. What this process involved was establishing the customer as the Service Integrator, creating the interface contracts, and building a Service Bridge.

To facilitate the customer role of Service Integrator, I divided up each process and the associated tasks that were performed; identifying them as either customer or vendor-related. I then invited the management of each area to attend a workshop where we all agreed to work together over a number of months. There was no shortcut to this process, and giving them an opportunity to contribute their input provided the necessary impetus and reasoning for them to buy into it.

CHAPTER 35

The Definition and Purpose of Service Modelling

Service Modelling involves building a relationship between the data and what people do with it. Understanding human behavior and 'getting ahead of the curve' by predicting the way in which data will be selected and entered allows for seamless management and integration of services. In addition, it minimises the impact of this information on the customer.

Having spent many years working in the IT industry, I have learned to always start with the end result in mind. I have developed a framework to model services for integration and management which can be applied to all businesses within any industry.

The purpose of service modelling is to drive IT from the Business perspective by creating a digital footprint of a service to support life-cycle management of this service. This is a complete flip-over of the way in which most IT people think and it involves using a guided method to teach them how to consider IT from a business person's perspective.

Assumptions of the Model

The key assumption of this model is that it must be led from the top. When all the data is collated, validated and related, it is presented to executives (or savvy business owners) with recommended options to improve the IT Infrastructure and Operation. During my career, I have found that developing an understanding of the big picture and having the data to support decisions and strategies has enabled me to sign-up for very large programs to drive these initiatives ... and to hit the target every time.

Process

The process used in the model involves a unique and dynamic method of collecting data attributes essential to service life-cycle management that, when shared and utilised, enable Service Integration and Management processes (among others) to operate efficiently and effectively. Essentially, digital lifecycle management involves only collecting the required data that will be maintained as part of the process itself.

Experiment

Over the years, I have experimented and tested service modeling in small, medium, large, and extra-large organisations (ranging from simple to complex). During this time, I have built a predictable solution for most business services and their underpinning IT systems. Generally, every organisation has approximately 26 core services so, as you can imagine, with the exception of a few vertical lines of business, they start to become predictable.

CHAPTER 36

Analysing the Results and Drawing Conclusions

After implementing and executing these modelling processes, I observed the data I collected and, over time, I discovered that it all started to look the same. Sure, there are anomalies sometimes; however, 80% of the available data was not presented in a way that made it useful.

My subsequent results have led to the development of an application that executives can use to facilitate data capture, monitor progress, and enable decision-making as soon as possible. I am able to analyse the data, then produce a summary report which gives an organisation-wide perspective of the data. The model specifically focuses on identifying capability gaps and possible shortfalls in the operations within an organisation.

The Service Model that I have developed incorporates the following artefacts:

1. Service Modelling Framework Policy Document

This defines the framework used to model *services* and their underpinning *technology*, along with the accountabilities and governance rules in creating and maintaining the relevant documents.

2. Taxonomy Policy Document

This defines the *common language* to be used in classifying incoming work that aligns to the Service Modelling Framework which, in turn, ultimately provides reporting that is decision-focused.

3. Classes and Attributes Sheet

This identifies the types and quantity of *data* to be collected and imported into your chosen tool or platform.

4. Service Data Sheet

This lists all the *Services* collected in a format ready to be imported into your chosen tool or platform.

5. Product Data Sheet

This lists all the *Products* collected in a format ready to be imported into your chosen tool or platform.

6. Infrastructure Data Sheet

This lists all of the *Infrastructure* collected in a format ready to be imported into your chosen tool or platform.

7. Service Delivery and Support Catalogue Data Sheet

This defines the relationships between Support, Services, Products and Infrastructure.

8. Service Catalogue Summary Report

This provides a final overview analysis of the capability, capacity, and criticality of the Services and Technology in your Service Catalogue.

For a Service Model to be successful, an organisation must have an Executive Sponsor who champions the data capture, validation, results and subsequent quality assurance steps to maintain it.

Conclusion

During the past few years, I have retired from Program and Project Management. These days, my focus is on building a platform of tools which will enable technology and business people to access *data* in such a way that they can use it to make or support technology decisions and ask the right questions. I have been using this methodology to successfully deliver great outcomes for leading companies. I now feel that all the knowledge I have accumulated over the years will be of benefit to the industry that is now called 'Service Integration and Management' by providing a platform to determine what success looks like and how to achieve outstanding results.

One of my chief philosophies in life is that gaining knowledge and learning is only useful if you can share it and so this book is a summary of my life experience in technology and business to date.

My hope is that readers will find my approach and methods thought-provoking. If this is the case and you have found any of the concepts I have covered in the pages of this book helpful to your situation, I encourage you to put them into practice and refine them according to your own style.

I continue to live and learn by adapting to change and the way I do things – my own transformation is never-ending. The one common theme that I constantly observe is that the data tells the story. Hidden within the data are the essential secrets to understanding the people, process, partners, projects and technology (which are the cornerstones of my 4PT Framework) and forming a baseline for transformation in your world.

Appendix

Summary of Projects and Lessons Learned

Effects of Change
Most techos don't consider the impact change has either upstream and downstream; it seems all too difficult to them to attempt to understand the bigger picture of the way in which everything is connected. Even the smallest change can cause an outage and the data supports the statement that 90% of major outages are caused by change. One of the key drivers associated with building a platform involved creating a procedure for techos to find out what is upstream and downstream from them. In this way, when they encounter a change, they are then able to identify its potential business impact and, while it would seem to be counter intuitive, communicate this information to the business users. I have seen techos under-estimate the impact of a change and over-estimate the control they have over how the technology layers will respond to the change. If you don't understand how things are interconnected then you cannot possibly know what will shift when you make a change or what impact it will have on the customer.

Evidence and analysis speak volumes

Providing an answer or demonstrating great skill doesn't necessarily guarantee Executive buy-in.

When you present the evidence (i.e. the data) with an analysis of what it means, you will usually elicit Executive interest. You get buy-in when the data and analysis supports their anecdotal knowledge which, in turn, forms a baseline and opens the door for a discussion about transformation.

Below the Executive level, the data often is often considered to be threatening as it exposes the weaknesses of the operation. Building a platform that enables executives to see gaps in capability has revolutionised my consulting business as it helps everyone to agree on what to focus on.

Sometimes the business benefits are not realised!

While working in some organisations, I observed how challenging it was to run effective programs over multiple years and achieve the Return on Investment (ROI) that underpins the entire business case that initially financed the program. As a result, I started to create benefits that could be realised over shorter timeframes and became creative about turning business benefits into financial outcomes (savings or revenue).

It is crucial to establish the baseline of the current state, know your starting position, track performance to this baseline and keep all of the stakeholders involved accountable. Being able to deomonstrate the traceability of benefits, their realisation and all the risks involved extending beyond Technology into the Business operation ensures responsibility is shared across multiple people and is not just of the jurisdiction of the Program Manager.

Fixing things one at a time

Documentation and manuals seem to be the most under-utilised asset available to IT people. I have always been passionate about gaining knowledge by reading documentation and manuals. I was mainly motivated by the fact that I didn't want to repeat the same thing twice and I imagined that customers felt the same way. Ensuring that the Helpdesk had the necessary knowledge and giving them confidence to solve issues over the phone seemed to me to be a winning formula.

Building a platform that captures and relates the critical technology attributes required to run an Operation was the leanest approach to knowledge management I could find.

Recognising that IT people have an aversion to communicating with others by writing and sharing, it is critical to make the capture and maintenance of knowledge as quick and simple as possible.

Rather than the traditional knowledge management approach, we started to 'think outside the box'. Once the Helpdesk have the necessary knowledge as well as a classification system (taxonomy) in place, they feel more confident about talking to customers and fixing issues over the phone.

The power of team and testing

When planning new programs or projects, invariably a discussion about reducing the budget or shortening the timeline takes place. Many times during this discussion a question about testing will arise and why three iterations are required. I always ensure that I explain why it is easier to shorten the timeline when the testing goes well rather than experience the impact and disappointment of extending the timeline if the testing goes badly. My goal is to make sure the project ends up involving three cycles of testing.

Business Process Mapping

Providing a visual version of the methodology and standard template ensured that the whole team felt confident their contribution would make a difference. By involving everyone and canvasing their viewpoint, I felt confident that nothing would be missed.

Taking a data approach made it easier and much quicker to collate and consolidate the information and summarise the overall Business Unit. The advantage for the managers and Executive was that they now had an overview which they could use to drill down to inspect areas which I'd tagged as potential candidates for improvement.

How workflow can protect data

I am never surprised to find this level of detail is overlooked when the IT department implements applications themselves. Over the years, I have taught many people how to deliver functional requirements through a document called a Functional Specification (which covers requirements, design and use cases).

Getting the team together with those stakeholders who will use the system and walking through each function does take time. However, it makes all the difference by ensuring that there are no assumptions or areas open to misinterpretation. I also noticed that when the team members understand the project goals, they are able to come up with improvements by providing different options. The best way for them to do this is via a prototype. All Service Integration and Management tools have a multitude of options and finding the most appropriate one is the key to matching the technology with the people capability.

The Redbook and the Hot Seat in action

As the manager of the Service Centre, my responsibility was to create an opportunity for the technical gurus to become familiar with the Service Centre operation, including answering the phone and providing valuable knowledge.

The mutual respect and relationships that were built as a result of this collaborative interaction between the Service Centre people and the technical gurus increased the fix on first outcomes up to 90%, reduced escalations and led to an enormously cohesive team.

How non-IT people view technology

You cannot assume anything about the way data is created without watching the behaviour of the people creating it. What is even more astounding is noting what drives human behavior when they interact with a system.

With every new project I undertake I make an effort to observe it in action so that I don't assume anything when I come to analyse the data. I can then see the correlation between the data quality and human behavior. It is only at this point that I will attempt to resolve the root cause – human behavior.

Right people in the right roles

One of the key characteristics I look for in a person is their ability to communicate well. A common comment I get from technical people is 'I don't have time to communicate because I'm too busy trying to fix the problem'. On the whole, poor customer service stems from a lack of willingness to communicate. For most people, this really means that they need to over communicate. I lead by example and demonstrate to people many ways of communicating effectively and how this, in turn, creates trust and integrity.

Customer versus vendor

Sometimes the customer is the actual problem and you can only help them when they are desperate. The rest of the time they are looking for someone to blame for internal issues within their business. I really came to understand the saying: 'The fish stinks from the head down'! I know this analogy is not very eloquent but it does express an inherent truth. Solving technology issues is easy for me; however, educating executives who are not technically-minded ... that can be very challenging!

People create the data

I have found that having a focus on the analytics (data and reporting) has always paid off. Often this process is not easy or doesn't occur quickly and I would encounter resistance along the way. However, embedding it into an organisation's culture is a great foundation for any operation. I consider being able to demonstrate a commitment to measuring and improving performance to be good governance. One of the associated benefits was instilling confidence in and gaining trust from the Executive and the customers.

Data analysis is the key skill

Gathering data from different organisations and then comparing them allows you to gather the best from both worlds. Preparing for and achieving significant change is as much about the buy-in of the associated people. If there is a science behind the change, your people will be more accepting, be more likely to be involved in the change and help to drive the outcomes. Ensuring that there is no loss in capability across multiple organisations would appear to me to be the ultimate plan.

All types of data are useful

This statement does not just apply to the Service Centre; it applies to all resources that deliver support services to a customer. When you start to really measure productivity levels within an organisation, you can be more realistic about staff numbers as a result of gaining insight into what the customer is experiencing. Whenever the customer satisfaction level is low I always investigate the staff roster but, more importantly, how closely it is adhered to.

In some cases, I have observed resource productivity levels as low as 50% and when I have put the data together to confirm this percentage, everyone looks surprised. I see this as being a starting position and I then implement actions to increase this level. When people see the science behind the numbers, it is amazing how quickly productivity improves without any change required. To me, this continues to validate that people are not really measuring or they have no trust with regards to the measurements.

Problems occur when Managers aren't aware of what their team is doing

As soon as I start to feel that someone is not the right person for the job I have been proven to be right. I recommend that you follow this instinct and never leave it too long to act or everyone will suffer. Every time I have left this scenario alone, I have always looked back and wished I had done something sooner. When I have been driven by the health of the team and have felt responsible about making the tough decisions, the team ends up being the healthiest it can be. I live my life according to the motto: 'If you don't change something then nothing changes'.

Mapping and Service Integration

It takes months to develop a process in an organisation in which the process spans all of the capabilities (towers) in the IT department, as well as the vendor. I was aware of how differently each person viewed the same process and the different ways in which it affected them.

To embed the process within an organisation involves a strategic sales and marketing exercise. It requires significant engagement on the part of every manager and their team to agree to change the way they are currently doing things. Quality measures and assurance that a process was being followed occurred as a result of having key outputs which the leadership team could inspect. Over time, this process gradually translated into the new way of doing things.

I found integrating vendors to be a much easier exercise. In situations where the customer takes responsibility for their 'Service Model' and defines exactly what data they need from a vendor and how they want that data to be delivered, vendor/s are usually willing to comply Within the customer environment, this specialist skill is often scarce.

For the past three years, I have focused on creating a standard 'Service Model' that customers can customise over time. I believe that helping customers to establish this core capability is the future direction of technology.

Data walkthroughs underpin service levels

In all the projects I worked on in which there were service levels involved, I ensured I was included at the beginning, during the discussion and at the end to make sure that they arrived in shape to be operationalised.

Baseline data creates realistic outcomes

Even a small degree of improvement can change the mood and tempo of a transformation. Without an established starting position, progress cannot be measured which, in turn, is the biggest killer to momentum and motivation I have witnessed. Many transformations lead to failure due to not establishing this critical baseline and once you are underway there is no going back. People forget quite quickly how things used to be once they have implemented a change in procedure. Without the data, there is no evidence or reference point.

It is amazing how few people are clear about the scope and performance of the area in which they operate. I will always start a project with the basics: how many people work in the department; do they have a job description; do they have performance objectives; and do they all work in the position that matches their job description or their skillset.

Reviewing basic personnel data provides an indication of an organisation's culture and where they are in terms of measuring this information. It also is an indicator of how much work will be required to initiate change and to work through resistance to the project. There is a relationship between culture and the project timeline, and this must be factored into the project plan and schedule.

Many projects produce great deliverables. However, the real success of any project lies in the transition from project into business as usual and the realisation of the transformational benefits.

Operations versus Projects

Due to rapid advances in technology and ever-increasing expectations, it became necessary for Operations people to juggle Operations and Projects. I observed that most people found this to be a huge challenge – possibly beyond their capabilities – and they were not able to successfully work in both Operations support and Projects.

I never assume that Operations Managers and Team Leaders will know how to lead and manage resources to deliver both operational activities and project deliverables. I ensure resources are assigned to the project at set weekly times to ensure that there is no slippage or miscommunication regarding what is expected. There are some people who can in fact juggle activities and meet deadlines; this is always a nice surprise when it happens.

Taking this procedure one step further – when the operational team find the work to be interesting and fun they can become the best champions for the project. They can dispel any friction or resistance to the change that occurs as a result of technology transformation by leveraging their relationships on both sides of the fence.

Use data to test and retest until ITIL is operational

Joining the data dots between the people, process, partners, projects and technology is critical to the success of operationalising ITIL, and of the project overall. Although at times the data can seem overwhelming, when each person takes responsibility for their part, it makes it easier to manage the data quality.

It all comes down to the training

This may sound old-fashioned but I won't conduct training of Operations people unless their manager or team leader attends as well – every session. I have experienced some terrible training sessions where I have asked trainees to leave because they seemed to be incapable of participating without focusing on the negatives.

I also found other benefits from following this practice. Many managers and team leaders don't work that closely with their team members, particularly if they work in a highly technical area or don't share the same technical background. This is also the case if they are not co-located and they don't socialise outside of work. Consequently, training can be an opportunity for them to get to know their people and the way they behave outside the work environment.

Over the years, I have built simulation games that I incorporate into training sessions to make the process a little more hands-on. I have found that this has helped to lighten what can at times be a dry subject.

As a final note, I always measure people's attendance at training sessions and have a rule in place that everyone must complete the training program – no exceptions. We always schedule in make-up sessions at the end of the planned training program to cater for those people who were sick, on holidays or away from work for any reason. In addition, there is a group who may have had to attend to operational issues on the training days. I provide a report to the executives listing everyone's name and where we didn't get 100% attendance at training, the names of those people who were absent from the session.

About the Author

With 30 years' experience in the Australian IT industry, Christine McNamara is passionate about making critical business goals possible through technology. Christine has worked for many leading organisations, both locally and abroad.

Christine delivers real business benefits while saving customers valuable time and money; seemingly impossible technology projects are her speciality. Her ability to tailor technology solutions to meet customers' requirements has made her a sought-after IT and business consultant. Known as a straight shooter, Christine has a reputation for getting the job done while exceeding customers' expectations.

www.ingramcontent.com/pod-product-compliance
Lightning Source LLC
Chambersburg PA
CBHW070401200326
41518CB00011B/2022